Creative Cooking & Eating In A Garlic Free Zone

Delicious food for we who can't eat garlic, and you who choose not to.

Christine Sutton

Copyright 2022 © Christine Sutton

All rights reserved. No part of this publication may be reproduced, distributed or transmitted in any form or by any means without prior written permission.

Christine Sutton

Cooking & Eating in a Garlic-Free Zone

First published 2022 by M.C. Sutton, 139/218 Bishop Rd, Beachmere, Queensland, Australia

Editor Chris Sutton

ISBN 978-0-6451879-3-9

Introduction

Let me be very clear, this book is not for the allium *allergic*.

It is for those who are garlic and onion intolerant, or who dislike garlic.

Garlic and onion (allium) are a little known and even less recognised member of the food intolerance and allergy family. Restaurants cater for gluten, nut, sesame, shellfish, dairy and egg intolerances, vegetarians and vegans, but almost every dish on a restaurant menu contains garlic in some form or another. Food manufacturers' lists of ingredients hide garlic in 'herbs and spices', or list garlic powder, dried garlic and garlic as one of the normal ingredients.

The recipes in this book have been adapted or created for use by those who cannot or choose not to eat garlic. They are all garlic free. Some are also onion free. *They are not necessarily FODMAP friendly recipes.* They may not suit those with other IBS or anaphylaxis triggers.

I am not a medical specialist, a dietician or an allergist. I do not claim to be an authority on Irritable Bowel Syndrome or FODMAP diets. Nor am I a chef. I'm simply a passionate cook and all round lover of fantastic, flavourful food, who, out of sheer frustration, put my skills to work to solve a problem.

These recipes are dishes that I created or adapted as a work-around for my personal garlic intolerance. I find them safe for me, and for friends who share my allium intolerance.

The substitutes for garlic listed here have been researched over the years through various highly respected and trusted IBS specialist organisations. The sources are listed at the back of the book.

I hope those of you in the same boat as I am will find something to tickle your taste buds in this book. If you do, and if you become confident enough to adapt your own favourite dishes to be garlic free, I've achieved my goal to give you food that you can enjoy, and the tools to create your own garlic free foodie heaven.

Dedication

To Paul, who carefully reads every label on packaged or tinned food for me. Despite your Italian heritage, you have cooked and eaten garlic free with me over a period of more than 20 years. I can tell how much you miss it, as whenever I go away, I return to a man with a huge smile on his face and a house reeking of garlic. I love you and appreciate your support.

To all garlic intolerant foodies like me who know the frustrations and pain of being unable to find garlic-free products, menu choices and recipes. You should have wider choices than between the bland and the bloating. You deserve to eat great food. This book is for you!

To Monash University FODMAP Team - your research and information has been invaluable in helping me to understand my food intolerance and find substitutes for garlic and onions. Thank you.

To George and all those chefs and cooks who have gone out of their way to find garlic free solutions for me without suggesting "a grilled chicken breast and salad, no dressing". I wish there were more like you, and that all chefs offered garlic free deliciousness in their restaurants and cafes as a normal choice on the menu. We who can't or choose not to eat garlic are so very grateful.

To those food manufacturers who have listened to the research and are producing accessible pre-prepared food that is FODMAP friendly and therefore free of garlic and onions. Please continue. We need you.

To *Woolworths and Coles Supermarkets* who have product ingredients listed on their online shopping websites, allowing us to find onion and garlic free products without having to read the oh-so-tiny print on cans and packages. Both retailers carry FODMAP products bearing the FODMAP symbol. Thank you.

Acknowledgements

Monash University FODMAP website, a constant source of up-to-date information, resources and ideas.

The many great chefs and cooks whose books, TV shows and websites provide the constant impetus for me to create, adapt, and re-imagine fantastic food - allium free.

Every time I see you load a dish with garlic, I am inspired to prove that all food can be simply delicious, while remaining accessible to those of us who have to live in a garlic-free zone.

FOREWORD

I was in my mid-50s when I realised there was a problem. Every now and again, for no apparent reason, I spent several days running to the bathroom; stomach cramps, bloating, diarrhoea, headaches and terrible fatigue. To track down the cause I kept a food diary, a list of everything I ate over a few months. A pattern emerged. Every time I ate Greek, Indian, Asian or Italian food, my body reacted. Tests, and an elimination diet followed. A few months later, I had an answer. I had become garlic intolerant.

The fructans in garlic create a reaction in my body similar to Irritable Bowel Syndrome (IBS). While relatively rare in the total population, there are many folks like me, some of whom have a reaction to all alliums, and some who are allergic to them to the extent of life-threatening anaphylaxis.

The only way for me to avoid illness is to avoid garlic, in any form. I had to learn to eat differently. It's when you find out who your staunch friends are and which chefs are aware of food intolerance. Genuine friends and brilliant cooks don't get huffy and offended when I ask the question "Is there garlic in this?". Those who know me don't need to ask, they warn me first. To be fair, it isn't their fault. In Australia, garlic and onion aren't yet recognised as allergens. Everyone knows about wheat, dairy, egg, nut and shellfish allergies and intolerances, few know about garlic and onions.

Even ingredients can be an issue. Manufacturers invariably print the ingredient labels in teeny-tiny print. (I receive some strange looks when I use my iPhone to photo the labels in order to enlarge them.) Almost every manufactured or take-away food contains garlic in some form. There are some manufacturers and supermarkets who are on the ball and list the ingredients in the product description on their online store, but they are few. We have work to do there.

When I first learned about my intolerance, the chef at my favourite Greek restaurant was also a good friend, and so supportive. He called me his 'favourite vampire'. I could simply say "Feed me!" and out would come wonderful food; no garlic or onions, bursting with flavour - and safe. It was he who inspired me to experiment with my own recipes. Over the years, I have created and adapted recipes to suit my need for a garlic free diet and without having to put up with boring, bland meals.

Now, it's time to share them, and the garlic free foodie tricks I've adapted, created and learned over the years. Whether you are fructan intolerant, or just don't like to eat garlic, or if you are the kind and thoughtful friend of a garlic intolerant person, this book is for you.

Happy garlic free cooking,
Chris Sutton

CONTENTS

Cooking without garlic	**10**
Substitutes for garlic	**11**
Why is garlic infused oil okay?	12
Spices that add flavour	13
Weights, measures and conversions	14
Metric Conversions	15
Baking tin & dish sizes (cm to inches)	16
The Golden Rules	17
Basic stocks	**18**
GaF Chicken stock	18
GaF Rich Beef stock	19
Seafood/Fish stock	20
Prawn stock	20
Basic Condiments	**21**
GaF Basil Pesto	21
Basil Pesto (Garlic Infused Oil, no cheese)	21
GaF Dijon Mustard	22
GaF Worcestershire Sauce (Contains onions)	22
GaF Thai Satay (Peanut) Sauce	23
GaF BBQ Sauce	23
Mayonnaise	24
Seafood Sauce (Mum's GaF version)	24
Old Family Favourites	**25**
The Best Fish Pie Ever	26
Chicken Wings	27
Chicken Chasseur	28
Meat Loaf	29
Nanna's Green Tomato Chutney	30
Absolutely delicious. Contains Onion.	30
Rissoles in Gravy	31
Nanna's Homemade Sausage Rolls	32
Easy Tomato Ketchup	33
Dauphinoise Potatoes	34

Mediterranean 35

    The Mediterranean Pantry 36
    Yarithes 39
    Bolognese Sauce 40
    Basil and Pesto Salad 41
    Mushroom & Thyme Linguine 42
    Leek & Mushroom Risotto 43
    Pumpkin & Goat's Cheese Lasagne 44
    Minestrone my way 46
    Chicken Cacciatore 47
    Moussaka 48
    Veal and Mushroom Pasta 50
    Roast Chicken Italian Style 51
    Lamb Souvlaki 52
    Keftedes 54
    Greek Salad 56
    Lemon, Basil and Oil Marinade/Dressing 56

Indian 57

    The Indian Pantry 58
    Indian Cottage Pie 59
    Alu Gobi 60
    Alu Gosht 61
    Chicken Biryani 62
    Naan Bread 64
    Chicken Korma 66
    Cucumber Raita 67
    Tandoori Chicken 68

Asian 69

    Essentials for Asian Cooking 70
    Korean dumplings 72
    Steamed Barramundi and Mushroom Rice 73
    Vietnamese Prawn Spring Rolls 74
    Thai Coconut Soup 76
    Garlic Free Red Curry Paste 76
    Beef in Oyster Sauce 77
    Prawn Chow Mein, Soft Noodles 78
    Malay Prawn Soup 79

Garlic Free Hoisin Sauce	80
Garlic Free Gochujang Paste	80
Korean Bibimbap	81
Prawn Wontons	83
Green Rice Crusted Prawns & Plum Sauce	84

Middle Eastern — **85**

Essential Middle Eastern Ingredients	86
Baharat	88
Za'atar	88
Baked Fish Lebanese Style	89
Beef Fatteh	90
Baba Ganoush	91
Prawn Börek	93
Morrocan Chicken Tagine	94
What is a tagine	95
Hummus	96
Beetroot Hummus	96
Felafels	97
Cabbage Rolls	98

Your Own Recipes — **99**

Resources, Useful Websites, and Attributions — **105**

Resources	106
Useful Websites	106
Attributions	107

THE BASICS
GARLIC FREE

Cooking without garlic

Let me repeat, this is a book for those who are garlic and onion intolerant or who don't like garlic.
Not **for the allium allergic.**

I am not a doctor, or a dietician or a food allergies specialist or any kind of medical specialist at all. However, I learnt in my mid 50s there are things called fructans present in the allium (onion) family that are responsible for the gastric disaster that follows my consumption of garlic and sometimes onions *in any form whatsoever* and it's best that I avoid them.

I'm lucky. I'm not **allergic** to garlic or onions. I certainly won't have an anaphilactic reaction and possibly die. I just spend several days in the bathroom and very unwell. I won't describe the symptoms - too gross - but those afflicted with this intolerance will know exactly what's happening!

Over the last twenty odd years I've learnt the best solution is simply to adapt my normal food and recipes and cook them without garlic, and often without onions. Hopefully the lessons I've learned in how to do this will encourage you to give it a try.

It's not hard. Just make sure the right ingredients are in your pantry and follow the recipes. Then try it yourself in baby steps, one substituted ingredient at a time.

As we go, I'll give you some tips on where to look for hidden garlic, and where to find various substitute foods for things like Italian cold meats that are cured with garlic marinades. You'll also find some basic recipes in this section for staple ingredients like pesto and stocks to use in the main recipes sections.

Remember, everyone's tolerance of foods is different, so it is always best to test out some of these strategies yourself and see if you are able to tolerate them.

I have adapted and created these recipes over 25+ years of garlic intolerance. All of them are garlic free.

Some give you the option of using garlic infused oil as a substitute for garlic, others do not. It is an optional ingredient for those that like the garlic flavour.

Many are garlic and onion free and list the green tops of leeks and spring onions as a safe, tasty substitute for onion.

The recipes range from good old fashioned Aussie family favourites to those from the major cuisines of the world. They are dishes that usually contain garlic. You will come across them in restaurants, cookbooks, magazines, in Granny's notebooks and online. They were off the menu for me and my family for a long time.

I hope that you will try different ways of preparing garlic-free meals using these recipes as a guide.

I also hope that if you are successful, you will take the bit between your teeth and go to your recipe books and adapt some of your favourites from there, using the guidelines in this book.

substitutes for garlic

No unrelated vegetable has quite the same taste as onions or garlic, but some aromatics that may be good options for garlic substitution include:

- **Fennel** has a licorice-like taste but onion-like texture. Try it with chicken or fish.
- **Celery** is among the most common aromatics.
- **Capsicum** is often used in Cajun cooking. Green capsicum and celery are a good base for rice dishes or savoury stews.
- **Carrots** are used as an aromatic in French cooking in combination with celery.
- **Celeriac,** or celery root, is the knobby root of one variety of celery. Peeled and diced, it can be used as an aromatic in sauces or stews.

Herbs and Spices

- *Asafoetida* is a spice from India with a very strong smell that, when added to warm oil, tastes much like garlic and onions. You need only a sprinkle, as it's very strong. Try a pinch per person, e.g. a dish that serves 4 would require 4 pinches of asafoetida.
- Garlic chives, an herb with a garlicky flavour, are an obvious substitute, although they may be a problem for onion intolerance.
- Peppercorns—white, pink, or Szechuan—can add different flavors to your cooking.
- Cumin's distinctive taste may work well in some recipes, especially those in which where garlic is used raw.
- Ginger and galangal have distinctive flavours but can add to stir-fries as aromatics.

Infused Oil

Garlic-infused oil is fine, as the fructans are not fat-soluble. You can buy infused oil or sauté whole garlic cloves in oil and discard the solids before using it in your dish. I have found that the garlic infused oil produced by Cobram, is safe for me. It's quite strong. I use only a few drops and make up the rest of the recipe's oil needs with plain olive oil.

FODMAP Friendly Foods

Foods that are safe for for people who suffer with Irritable Bowel Syndrome, including those of us with a garlic/onion intolerance, are marked with the FODMAP logo. Most foods with the logo are produced by specialist food suppliers. However, there are well-known manufacturers that have started to add FODMAP approved foods to their range of products. I have found;

- **Cobram**, have an approved garlic infused oil
- **Raguletto** Italian herbs pasta sauce
- **Val Verde** and **Mutti** passata. I use the Mutti passata regularly - it's delicious.

While the symbol denotes that the product has approval as a low FODMAP food, that may not always denote it is garlic and/or onion free. Look for Garlic and Onion Free on the label.

Check the ingredients on the label, very carefully. This particularly applies to foods like potato chips and sauces - the flavoured ones often have garlic powder in the flavourings. Bad news!!! Keep looking, and where you can, support the producers who are trying to support us.

Why is garlic infused oil okay?

It's okay because the fructans that create the reactions in your intolerant body are not soluble in oil. If you cook a clove whole in oil, and then remove it before you continue cooking, you will have the flavour but none of the nasties.

Australia's Monash University has a team of FODMAP experts who constantly research and disseminate information about IBS.

I highly recommend that you explore their website, it's full of great information and help. They can explain better than I why garlic oil is fine for most people who are garlic intolerant.

> *"The fructan content in onion and garlic are soluble in water. This means that if you put onion or garlic into a soup or stock, some of the fructan content will leach out into the water.*
>
> *Therefore the strategy of putting a whole onion or garlic clove into a soup and then pulling the pieces out before consuming the soup will not work, as the fructan content will have already leached into the water.*
>
> *In an oil based dish the fructans will not leech out (as fructans are not soluble in oil). Therefore, if you are making something based in oil, for example a stir-fry, it is possible to add a large piece of onion or a whole garlic clove and simply pull the pieces out before adding other ingredients. This way you will have the flavour without the fructan content leaching into the meal.*
>
> *The other alternative that works very well to get some flavour into your cooking is using the green parts of spring onion or chives as a replacement for onion. When using these alternatives, keep in mind that they won't need to be sautéed for as long as regular onion and you may prefer to add them into the pot later in the cooking process to get maximum flavour from them. For some garlic flavour you can make your own garlic infused olive oil which you can use in your cooking instead of your regular oil. The Indian spice Asafoetida powder can also be used as a spice to replace onion flavour and you can buy this from an Indian supermarket (be careful when using it as it has a potent smell).*
>
> *Remember that everyone's tolerance to foods is different, so it is always best to test out some of these strategies yourself and see if you feel that you are able to tolerate them."*

(Low FODMAP Diet | IBS Research at Monash University - Monash FODMAP, 2021)

Spices that add flavour to various cuisines

While many of the following cuisines incorporate garlic in the recipes, removing it does not necessarily remove the character or flavour of the dish.

Experiment by adding another herb or spice from the list to create your own deliciousness.

French Thyme, nutmeg, rosemary, sage, tarragon, black pepper, saffron, parsley, lavender, dill, bay leaves

Italian Parsley, basil, bay leaves, sage, thyme, rosemary, oregano, marjoram

Greek Oregano, mint, dill, basil, fennel, rocket, marjoram, purslane, rosemary, cinnamon, cumin, and coriander.

Spanish Saffron, paprika, bay leaf, rosemary, parsley, thyme, chilli, pimento, cayenne pepper (a good substitute for chilli), oregano,

Mexican Coriander, cumin, paprika, cinnamon, chilli, black pepper, cloves

Asian Asian chives, chilli, coriander, fenugreek, lemongrass, mint, pandan leaves, Thai basil, cardamom, cloves, cumin, fennel seeds, star anise, turmeric, five spice, sesame seeds, cinnamon, ginger, galangal, kaffir lime leaves

Indian/Sri Lankan Fennel seeds, asafoetida, chilli, cardamom, black pepper, cumin, capers, bay leaves, cinnamon, cloves, coriander, curry leaves, curry powder, fenugreek, goraka, ginger, mint, mustard seeds, nutmeg, poppy seeds, saffron, sesame seeds, tamarind, turmeric, basil, lemongrass, rampa leaves

Middle Eastern Bay leaves, black pepper, cardamom, cinnamon, cloves, coriander, cumin, fennel, ginger, coriander seed, allspice, mint, fenugreek, paprika, parsley, sesame seeds, thyme, turmeric, nutmeg, chilli, saffron.

Weights, measures and conversions

This book incorporates current Australian metric weights and measures Before we start, you need to be able to decipher the recipes - so here's a guide to the abbreviations, measurements and conversions that you may need to cook from this book, or from other cookbooks you might use to adapt their recipes to garlic free cooking.

Abbreviations

Sometimes a recipe may be measured in grams and kilograms - gm & kg, (Metric), ounces and pounds- oz & lb (Imperial), or cups and spoons.

gm / g = gram	ml = millilitres	" = inch
kg = kilogram	L = litre	cm = centimetre
oz = ounce	tspn = teaspoon	sml = small
lb = pound	dstpn = dessertspoon	med = medium
	tblspn / tbls = tablespoon	lge = large
GaF = Garlic Free	OF = Onion Free	

To make it easier for you to be successful, here's a chart or two. You can use them to convert from our Australian metric to old Imperial measures and Australian cups to US cup, which are slightly different.

There is a slight difference between Australian/UK cups and USA cups.

For most recipes, the difference is small and won't affect the finished dish.

When baking from an American recipe, you can remove 2 teaspoons from each cup measure to quickly get from Australian to US measures.

	Australian	US
1 cup	250 mls	240 mls
½ cup	125 mls	120 mls
¼ cup	60 mls	60 mls

Australian/UK Cup	Metric
1/4 cup	60ml
1/3 cup	80ml
1/2 cup	25ml
1 cup	250ml

Metric Conversions

Liquids

Metric	Cup	Imperial
30ml		1 fl oz
60ml	¼ cup	2 fl oz
80ml	⅓ cup	2 ¾ fl oz
100ml		3½ fl oz
125ml	½ cup	4 fl oz
150ml		5 fl oz
180ml	¾ cup	6 fl oz
200ml		7 fl oz
250ml	1 cup	8 ¾ fl oz
310ml	1¼ cups	10½ fl oz
375ml	1½ cups	13 fl oz
430ml	1¾ cups	15 fl oz
475ml		16 fl oz
500ml	2 cups	17 fl oz
625ml	2 ½ cups	21½ fl oz
750ml	3 cups	26 fl oz
1L	4 cups	35 fl oz
1.25L	5 cups	44 fl oz
1.5L	6 cups	52 fl oz
2L	8 cups	70 fl oz
2.5L	10 cups	88 fl oz

Weights

Metric	Imperial
10g	¼oz
15g	½oz
30g	1oz
60g	2oz
90g	3oz
125g	4oz (¼ lb)
155g	5oz
185g	6oz
220g	7oz
250g	8oz (½ lb)
280g	9oz
315g	10oz
345g	11oz
375g	12oz (¾ lb)
410g	13oz
440g	14oz
470g	15oz
500g	16oz (½ kg) (1 lb)
750g	24oz (1½ lb)
1kg	32oz (2 lb)
1.5kg	48oz (3 lb)

 # Baking tin & dish sizes (cm to inches)

Recipe Calls For	Volume	Use Instead
1 (20 x 4)cm round cake tin	4 cups	1 (8 x 4)-inch loaf tin;
2 (20 x 4 cm) round cake tin	8 cups	2 (8 x 4-inch) loaf tins; 2 (9-inch) round cake tins; 1 (10-inch) springform tin
1 (23 x 4 cm) round cake tin	6 cups	1 (8-inch) round cake tin; 1 (8 x 4-inch) loaf tin; 1 (11 x 7-inch) baking dish
2 (23 x 4 cm) round cake tin	12 cups	2 (8 x 4-inch) loaf tins; 1 (9-inch) tube tin; 2 (8-inch) round cake tins;
1 (38x26 cm) round cake tin	11 cups	2 (8-inch) round cake tins; 1 (9-inch) tube tin; 1 (10-inch) springform tin
23 cm tube tin	12 cups	2 (9-inch) round cake tins; 2 (20 cm) round cake tins;
28x17 cm baking dish	6 cups	1 11 x 7 x 2-inch baking dish; 1 (9-inch) square baking dish; 1 (9-inch) round cake tin
8 x 4-inch loaf tin	6 cups	1 (8-inch) round cake tin; 1 (11 x 7-inch) baking dish
23 x 4 cm springform tin	10 cups	1 (10-inch) springform tin; 2 (20 cm) round cake tins; 2 (9-inch) round cake tins
25 cm springform tin	12 cups	2 (20x 10 cm) loaf tins 1 (9-inch) tube tin; 2 (9-inch) round cake tins; 1 (10-inch) round cake tin 2 (8-inch) round cake tins
20 cm square baking dish	8 cups	(23cm) deep dish pie plate; 1 (9 x 5-inch) loaf tin; 1 (8-inch) pie plate
23 cm square baking dish	8 cups	1 (11 x 7-inch) baking dish; 1 (9 x 2-inch) deep dish pie plate; 1 (9 x 5-inch) loaf tin; 2 (8-inch) pie plates

The Golden Rules

1. ENJOY COOKING!!! Get creative, experiment with the alternatives to garlic and onion and don't tell dinner guests that the dishes are garlic free - at least not until after they have complimented you on what a great cook you are! Then you can gloat.

2. Fresh is best! It is always preferable to make your own stocks and condiments from scratch. Make the stocks in bulk and freeze in 500 ml containers for use later. The recipes for the condiments are small amounts that will last for a while in the fridge.

3. If you must use bought stocks and condiments, read every label on frozen, canned, bottled and packaged food. Onion, garlic, shallot, spring onion and leek are often found in savoury products like soups, curry pastes, pasta sauces, marinated meats, flavour 'sachets' and simmer sauces. They may not be listed.

4. Because the onion family are not considered 'allergens' by Australian law, they do not have to be declared in plain English, and can hide as 'vegetable powder' or 'dehydrated vegetables'.

5. Watch out for ingredients listed as herbs, spices or flavourings, especially the ones that combine dried herbs and spices into a particular mixture, e.g. Mediterranean Seasoning, Italian Herbs and BBQ Rub.
   Avoid these, particularly if they are higher up the ingredient list.

6. When you start to use garlic infused oil, or the green tops of leek or spring onion, start in small amounts and see how you go. If you increase the amount, and you feel unwell, go back a step.

Basic stocks

A good stock takes a long time to reach its full flavour. The secret to a great stock is to cook it slowly, with the liquid just moving, over a number of hours. I learnt this method in the 1970s at a cooking class led by Serge Dansereau, then the Executive Chef at the Regent Hotel in Sydney. When I make my stocks, I put them on late in the afternoon and leave them cooking all night. The result is a clear, flavoursome stock that makes your food sing!!!

Hint! *Do not peel the vegetables, just wash them well.*

GaF Chicken stock

For vegetable stock, leave out the chicken.

Ingredients
6 fresh continental parsley stalks
4 fresh thyme sprigs
1.3kg whole chicken
4L cold water
3 dried bay leaves
3 celery sticks, coarsely chopped
1 Bulb of fennel coarsely chopped
2 large carrots, coarsely chopped
Green tops of 4 large spring onions sliced
1 leek, trimmed, thickly sliced
1tspn each ground cumin & yellow mustard seed
12 black peppercorns
1 tsp salt

Method
1. Tie the parsley and thyme together with a piece of unwaxed kitchen string or twine.
2. Place chicken in a large stockpot.
3. Pour over water.
4. Cover and bring to heat on a low setting until the water begins to move.
5. Add herbs, bay leaves, celery, carrot, fennel, spring onion tops, leek, peppercorns and salt.
6. Bring up to heat again so that the liquid is just moving (less than a simmer). Adjust the heat to keep it at that temperature.
7. Leave to cook uncovered, for 6 hours minimum (overnight is best).
8. Turn off the heat and allow to cool.
9. Use tongs and a slotted spoon to transfer the chicken to a colander over a large saucepan and collect any excess stock and reserve.
10. When drained, remove and discard skin and bones.
11. Shred chicken meat. Place in an airtight container. Store in fridge.
12. Pour reserved excess stock back into the stockpot.
13. Line a large sieve with muslin. (Alternatively, I use a new Chux cloth.)
14. Place over a large bowl. Carefully ladle broth into sieve and drain the liquid.
15. Discard solids left in sieve.
16. Cover the broth with a large plate or tea towel.
17. Place in the fridge overnight to set the fat. Next day, carefully remove and discard the layer of solid fat from the top of the broth.

The stock can be frozen for up to 3 months.

GaF Rich Beef stock

Ingredients

2 kg beef brisket bones
½ cup olive oil
2 large leeks
4 large spring onions, green tops only.
3 large carrots
2 stalks celery
½ cup chopped parsnip
1 large potato
2 large tomatoes
8 whole black peppercorns
2 tsp smoked paprika
1 tsp black mustard seed
2 bay leaves
1 tablespoon salt
1 tblspns fresh thyme leaves
2 sprigs rosemary
4 litres water

Method

1. Place the brisket bones in a roasting tray and pour over the olive oil.
2. Roast until browned.
3. Meanwhile, chop the potato, carrot, parsnip, leeks, celery and spring onion tops into 1 cm cubes.
4. Remove the bones to a large plate and pour the juices and oil into a large stockpot.
5. Add the chopped vegetables to the stockpot and, stirring constantly, gently sauce but do not brown. (Add more olive oil if necessary).
6. When vegetable are beginning to soften pour in the red wine and allow to reduce a little.
7. Pour over the water, adding more if necessary to cover the meat and vegetable.

It is important not to boil/simmer a stock. It results in a scum forming on the top. For the best result, adjust the heat to keep the liquid in the pot just moving.

8. Bring to heat on a low setting until the water begins to move.
9. Add and add the chopped tomato, herbs and spices and salt.
10. Bring up to heat again so that the liquid is just moving.
11. Leave to cook uncovered, for 6 hours minimum (overnight is best).
12. Turn off the heat and allow to cool.
13. Use tongs and a slotted spoon to transfer the beef bones and any chunks of beef to a colander over a large saucepan and collect any excess stock and reserve.
14. When drained, remove and discard bones.
15. Shred any meat. Place in an airtight container. Store in fridge.
16. Pour reserved excess stock back into the stockpot.
17. Line a large sieve with muslin. Alternatively, I use a new Chux cloth.
18. Place over a large bowl. Carefully ladle broth into the sieve and drain the liquid.
19. Discard solids left in sieve.
20. Bring the stock to a simmer and allow to reduce by a third to give maximum flavour.
21. Cover the broth with a large plate or tea towel.
22. Place in the fridge overnight to set the fat. Next day, use a metal spoon to carefully remove and discard the layer of solid fat from the top of the broth.

The stock can be frozen for up to 3 months in 500ml containers or alternatively, freeze in ice block trays then seal in clip-lock bags, using as many as needed for your recipes.

Seafood/Fish stock
Choose a large boned white fish for this stock, e.g. Snapper, cod

Ingredients

1.5 kg fish heads, bones, and trimmings
2 tablespoons unsalted butter
2 leeks, white part only, thinly sliced
1 carrot, chopped
1 stick celery, chopped
1 cup dry white wine
1L water
1 bouquet garni (thyme, parsley, oregano)
1 tsp fennel seeds
10 whole black peppercorns
3 thick slices of lemon

Allow to cool before storing in the refrigerator for up to a week, or keep in the freezer for up to 3 months.

Method

1. Wash fish in cold water and drain well.
2. Melt butter in a pan over low heat.
3. Add leeks, carrot, and celery
4. Cook until softened, 5 to 7 minutes.
5. Add fish, wine, and water and bring to a gentle simmer.
6. Skim if necessary.
7. Add bouquet garni, peppercorns, and lemon
8. Return to a simmer, uncovered, for 30 minutes
9. Strain stock into a bowl through a colander lined with cheesecloth.

Prawn stock
For prawn stir-fries and risotto. Don't throw away those prawn heads!!

Ingredients

1 tblspn peanut/vegetable oil
Heads & shells from at least 1 kg green prawns
2 cm piece fresh ginger, chop finely
3 large spring onions
1 teaspoon whole black peppercorns
3 sprigs fresh thyme
2 bay leaves
⅓ cup soy sauce
1 tblspn palm sugar
1 tomato skinned and deseeded
1 dstspn sesame oil
½ bulb fennel roughly chopped
400 ml water cold water
1 tsp fennel seeds
½ teaspoon black peppercorns
¼ tsp Chinese 5 spice powder

Method - in a large wok

1. Heat the oil.
2. Drop in the prawn, stir fry 3-5 mins tossing constantly.
3. Add ginger, cook until just softening.
4. Add spring onion, fennel, fennel seeds, 5 spice and tomato.
5. Keep tossing, cook 3-5 mins
6. Add the soy sauce and palm sugar, toss quickly then add the water.
7. Bring to a simmer, cook until the stock has reduced by ⅓
8. Strain through sieve lined with muslin/clean Chux
9. Return liquid to wok and bring back to slow simmer.
10. Add salt & pepper to taste.

Cool. Pour into ice cube tray. When frozen store cubes in a clip lock bag in the freezer to use when needed.

Basic Condiments

Most recipes for casseroles, sauces, stews, and gravies have a stock base, or call for various condiments to give them flavour.

If using a bought product, particularly stock, check the ingredients before you buy. Nine times out of ten it will list garlic in some form or the other. Even powdered garlic will create a reaction.

The following are basic recipes condiments that you can use that are GaF and will give you you the big flavours that you need to cook delicious food. They are base ingredients for some recipes in this book.

GaF Basil Pesto

Ingredients

¼ cup Pine nuts
1 cup Basil leaves fresh, firmly compacted
1 cup Spinach leaves fresh, firmly compacted
¼ cup Parmesan shredded
½ cup Olive oil
Salt and Pepper to taste

Method

1. Add spinach, basil and pine nuts to the food processor.
2. Whizz until roughly chopped and combined.
3. Add cheese. Mix again until well combined.
4. Pour half the oil into the mix and pulse once or twice.
5. Add the remaining oil and pulse again. Don't over mix.
6. Add salt and pepper as needed.

Basil Pesto (Garlic Infused Oil, no cheese)

Ingredients

1½ cups fresh basil leaves
¼ cup fresh chives
¼ cup pine nuts
2 tablespoons fresh lemon juice
¼ cup garlic-infused olive oil
Sea salt

Method

1. Place basil, chives, pine nuts, and lemon juice in a food processor.
2. Process until roughly chopped.
3. Continue to process while slowly adding olive oil until desired consistency is achieved.
4. Season with salt.

Use immediately after preparing, or freeze in ice cube trays until solid and transfer to a zip-top bag. Use within three months.

GaF Dijon Mustard

Ingredients

2 tablespoons brown mustard seeds
4 tablespoons yellow mustard seeds
⅓ cup white vinegar or apple cider vinegar
¼ cup dry white wine
1 tablespoon minced spring onion tops
¾ teaspoon salt
¼ teaspoon white pepper
pinch all spice
2 tspns honey

Method

1. Combine mustard seeds, salt, white pepper, all spice well.
2. Add spring onion and mix.
3. Add vinegar and white wine and mix thoroughly.
4. Cover with plastic wrap.
5. Refrigerate for at least 8 hours.
6. Add mix to blender and whizz until smooth.

Store in a small sealed jar in refrigerator.
Use within three months.

GaF Worcestershire Sauce (Contains onions)

Ingredients

2 tablespoons olive oil
2 large sweet onions, roughly chopped
½ cup tamarind paste
2 tablespoons minced ginger
2 jalapeños, seeds removed, minced
¼ cup anchovies, chopped
¼ cup tomato paste
2 whole cloves
2 tablespoons freshly cracked black pepper
½ cup maple syrup
1 cup molasses
3 cups white vinegar
1 cup dark beer (in Australia ask for Old Beer)
½ cup orange juice
2 cups water
1 lemon, thinly sliced
1 lime, thinly sliced

Method

1. Gather the ingredients.
2. Heat the olive oil in a large saucepan and sauté the onions until soft, about 7 minutes.
3. Add the tamarind paste, ginger, and jalapeños. Cook over medium-low heat for another 5 minutes.
4. Add the remaining ingredients and stir to combine.
5. Bring to a boil, then reduce the heat and simmer, stirring occasionally, for about 5 hours.
6. The sauce is done when it is thick enough to coat the back of a spoon.
7. Strain the Worcestershire sauce into glass bottles or jars, and refrigerate.
8. Use in your favorite recipes and enjoy.

Store in a sealed bottle/jar in the refrigerator for up to a month.

GaF Thai Satay (Peanut) Sauce

Ingredients

2 tbsp red curry paste (See Asian Section of this book)
¾ cup (180g) natural peanut butter, smooth
150ml coconut milk
¼ cup (50g) white sugar
2 tsp dark soy sauce
1 tsp salt
2 tbsp lime juice
¾ cup (185ml) water.

It is important to use a good peanut butter. The better known commercial peanut butters are too thick, making it necessary to use more water to bring the sauce to a pouring consistency - hence less peanut flavour. Health food stores stock pure/natural peanut butter without additives and thickeners.

Others, such as Bega or Kraft, will work, but the difference in flavour is worth the journey to the health food store.

Method

1. Place all ingredients in a saucepan over medium low heat.
2. Stir to combine.
3. Simmer, stirring every now and then, for 5 minutes.
4. Adjust consistency with water. The sauce should be slightly thick but pourable.

Serve poured over satay chicken/ beef/prawn sticks with jasmine rice

GaF BBQ Sauce

Ingredients

1 tablespoon extra-virgin olive oil
1 brown onion, finely chopped
1 cup tomato puree/passata
½ cup Bourbon/Jack Daniels Whisky
½ cup apple juice
2 tablespoons apple cider vinegar
1 tablespoon treacle
1 tablespoon GaF Dijon mustard ¬
2 teaspoons Tabasco®, or to taste.

*See Recipe opposite page.

Method

1. Place a small saucepan over medium heat.
2. Add the oil and onion.
3. Sauté for 5 minutes, or until the onion has softened and is starting to colour.
4. Add the remaining ingredients.
5. Bring to a simmer and cook for 10 to 15 minutes, stirring as necessary, until the sauce is starting to thicken and has reduced by half.
6. Once the sauce has cooled, process in a blender until smooth.

Bottle and keep in the refrigerator for up to 3 weeks.

Mayonnaise

Ingredients

Yolk of 2 large free-range eggs
1 tspn GaF Dijon mustard
500 ml Extra Virgin Olive Oil
2 tblspn white wine vinegar
½ lemon
Good grind of Himalayan Salt

Method

1. Whisk the egg yolks in a bowl
2. Add the mustard and whisk.
3. Very slowly add about half the oil whisking continuously until thickened.
4. Now whisk in 1 tblspn of vinegar
5. Gradually add the remaining oil, whisking continuously.
6. Season with good grind of salt, a squeeze of lemon juice and a little more vinegar if needed.
7. Store in a sterilised jar in the fridge for up to one week.

Seafood Sauce (Mum's GaF version)

Ingredients

1/2 cup Heinz Salad Cream
1 tblspn GaF Mayonnaise
1/4 cup thickened cream
2 tspns GaF Tomato Ketchup
Tspn Vanilla Ice Cream

Method

1. Put all ingredients in a deep jug
2. Whisk by hand until they are all combined and the sauce is creamy and thick. It should be a pale pink.
3. Add a little more ketchup if necessary.
4. Adjust to taste.

Fantastic with prawns, wonderful with crab or lobster.

Old Family Favourites

The Best Fish Pie Ever

An old fashioned recipe with a luxury twist. **Contains onion.**

Prep Time	Cook Time	Total Time	Servings
20 mins	2 hrs	2 hrs 20 mins	6

Ingredients

4 eggs
1 small onion, thickly sliced
3 cloves
2 bay leaves
600ml milk
300ml thickened cream
450g Flathead
225g smoked cod
250gm uncooked prawns shelled and deveined, cut in half crossways
8 scallops
100g butter
45g plain flour
5 tbsp freshly chopped flat-leaf parsley
Freshly grated nutmeg
Salt and freshly ground white pepper
1.25kg peeled floury potatoes
1 egg yolk
Cup of medium grated sharp cheddar cheese.

You will need a 2 litre, shallow ovenproof casserole dish. Alternatively, you can make individual servings in oval ramekins, placed on a dinner plate with vegetables on the side.

Method

1. Hard-boil the eggs for 8 mins, cool.
2. Put the onion slices in a large pan with the cloves, bay leaf, 450ml of the milk, the cream, cod and smoked fish.
3. Bring to the boil, simmer for 5 mins.
4. Add the prawns and scallops and cook a further 3 mins.
5. Lift the fish, prawns and scallops out onto a plate.
6. Strain the cooking liquor into a jug.

Make the filling

1. When the fish is cool enough to handle, break it into large flakes, remove and discard **all** the bones and the skin.
2. Spread the fish over the base of a shallow 2 litre ovenproof dish.
3. Scatter the prawns and scallops evenly over the fish layer.
4. Peel the eggs, cut into thick slices and arrange on top of the seafood.
5. Melt half the butter in a pan, add the flour and cook for 1 minute, stirring.
6. Take the pan off the heat and gradually stir in the reserved cooking liquor.
7. Return it to the heat and bring slowly to the boil, stirring all the time.
8. Leave it to simmer gently for 10 minutes to cook out the flour.
9. Remove from the heat once more, stir in the parsley and season with nutmeg, salt and white pepper.
10. Pour the sauce over the fish and leave to cool.
11. Chill in the fridge for 1 hour.

Meanwhile prepare the mash

12. Boil the potatoes for 15–20 minutes.
13. Drain, mash and add the rest of the butter and the egg yolk.
14. Season with salt and freshly ground white pepper.
15. Beat in enough of the remaining milk to form a soft spreadable mash.
16. Preheat the oven to 200°C.

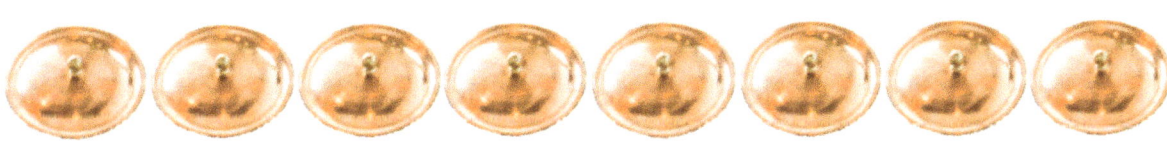

Assemble the dish

17. Spoon the potato over the filling and mark the surface with a fork.
18. Place in the oven and bake 30 mins.
19. Remove from the oven.
20. Scatter grated cheese across the top and return to the oven.
21. Bake until cheese melts and turns golden brown.

Serve with green vegetable on the side e.g. Peas, broccoli, asparagus, beans.

Chicken Wings
Sticky, sweet and soooo yummy.

Prep Time	Cook Time	Total Time	Servings
15 mins	45 mins	1 hr	4-6

Ingredients

12 whole chicken wings (or 24 mini drumsticks)
100ml light soy sauce
100ml honey
2 star anise
½ tspn ground cinnamon
3 star anise
¼ tspn ground cloves
1 tbs finely grated ginger
2 tsp sesame seeds, lightly toasted

Method

1. Preheat oven to 200C.
2. Rinse and dry the chicken wings.
3. Using a cleaver, remove the flat wing tip at the joint.
4. Separate the two parts of the wing at the joint between the 'mini drumstick' and the rest of the wing.
5. Place the chicken pieces in a large roasting dish.
6. Combine soy, honey, anise, cinnamon, ginger, and ⅓ cup (60ml) water and drizzle over the chicken.
7. Roast for 45 minutes, basting and turning often, until chicken is cooked through and sauce is reduced.
8. Remove star anise
9. Scatter with sesame seeds
10. Serve with a GaF dipping sauce.

Chicken Chasseur

Chicken the French way. Lovely! GaF but contains leeks

Prep Time	Cook Time	Total Time	Servings
10 mins	1 hr 50 mins	2 hrs	4

Ingredients

1 tsp olive oil
25g butter
4 chicken Marylands
2 medium leeks, cut crossways into 4 cm chunks
200g pack small button mushrooms
Handful of pitted black olives (optional)
225ml red wine
2 tbsp tomato purée
The leaves from 2 fresh thyme sprigs
500ml GaF chicken stock*

For this dish you need to use a lidded heat proof casserole that you can use on your cooktop or a large lidded frypan/skillet.

Method

1. Split each chicken Maryland into 2 pieces at the joint - leg and thigh.
2. Heat 1 tsp olive oil and half of the 25g butter in a large lidded frypan.
3. Season the chicken, fry for about 5 mins on each side until golden brown.
4. Remove and set aside.
5. Melt the remaining butter in the pan.
6. Add the onion, and fry for 5 mins until soft.
7. Add the mushrooms, cook for 2 mins.
8. Add 225ml red wine. Allow the alcohol to evaporate (1-2 mins)
9. Stir in tomato purée, let the liquid bubble and reduce for about 5 mins, then stir in the thyme and olives and pour in 500ml chicken stock.
10. Put chicken back into the pan, then cover and simmer on a low heat for about 1 hr until the chicken is very tender.
11. Remove the chicken from the pan and keep warm. Bring the sauce to a rapid boil and reduce the sauce for 10 mins or until it is syrupy and the flavour has concentrated.
12. Put the chicken pieces back into the sauce and serve. (1 leg and 1 thigh per person.)

Meat Loaf

Great old fashioned comfort food. Onion and garlic free

Prep Time	Cook Time	Total Time	Servings
10 mins	1.5 hrs incl standing	1 hr 40 mins	6

Ingredients

3 slices bread
1 large egg, lightly beaten
⅔ cup milk
1 cup shredded cheddar cheese
1 tblspn ground Nigella seeds
½ cup finely shredded carrot
½ cup frozen peas
1 teaspoon salt
¼ teaspoon pepper
1½ pounds ground beef

Glaze
¼ cup packed brown sugar
¼ cup passata
1 tablespoon GaF Dijon Mustard*

To cook for freezing.

1. Bake the meat loaf without glaze.
2. Allow to go cold.
3. Securely wrap cold meat loaf in foil, then freeze.
4. To use, partially thaw the meat loaf in the refrigerator overnight.
5. Prepare and spread glaze over top; reheat on a greased shallow baking pan in a preheated 180C oven until heated through.

Method

1. Preheat oven to 180C.
2. Tear bread into 5 cm pieces, place in a blender.
3. Cover and pulse to form coarse crumbs. Transfer to a large bowl.
4. Stir in egg, milk, cheese, nigella, carrot, peas, salt and pepper.
5. Add beef; mix lightly but thoroughly. Transfer to a greased 9x5-in. loaf pan.
6. In a small bowl, mix glaze ingredients; Spread over loaf.
7. Bake 60-80 minutes .
8. Stand 10 minutes before slicing.

The meatloaf can be frozen for later use.

*See condiments section

Nanna's Green Tomato Chutney

Absolutely delicious. Contains Onion.

Prep Time	Cook Time	Total Time	Servings
20 mins + overnight	1 - 1.5 hrs	1 hr 50 minutes	**4-6 x 250 ml jars**

Ingredients

1.5 kg green tomatoes chopped finely
2 cooking apples, peeled, cored and chopped finely
1 large onion chopped finely
2 tblspns salt
1 cup pitted prunes
¾ cup raisins
2 cups brown sugar
2 cups brown (malt) vinegar
1 cup Apple cider vinegar
1 inch piece fresh root ginger, grated
1 tspn Keen's Curry Powder*
1 tspn black peppercorns
4 cardamom pods
2 star anise
1 tspn coriander seeds.

Tie the peppercorns, cardamom, star anise and coriander seeds in a piece of muslin, or a small square of new Chux cloth tied with string.

You can replace the onion with celery or crushed nigella seeds.

Method

The day before cooking

1. Peel and chop tomatoes, apples and onions.
2. Place them in a non-metallic bowl and mix in the salt.
3. Allow to stand overnight.
4. Place the prunes in a bowl and cover with water. Stand overnight.

The next day

5. Drain the fruit and onion mix and the prunes.
6. Finely chop the prunes.
7. Put fruit, ginger, curry powder, raisins and prunes in a large pan.
8. Stir well to combine
9. Add the bag of spices and the rest of the ingredients to the pan
10. Bring to the boil, stirring to ensure the sugar dissolves.
11. Lower the heat and simmer, stirring every now and then, until thick. (approx 1 hr but keep an eye on it.)
12. Remove the spice bag and discard.
13. Pack into sterilised jars . Cover the jars with a tea towel until cool.
14. Seal the jars with a clean, sterilised lid.

Chutney is best left in a cool, dark pantry cupboard for at least 2 weeks before using. This allows the flavours to mature.

Once opened, keep in the fridge. Will keep for 6 weeks without spoiling. Unopened it can stay in a cool dark cupboard for 3 months.

*Other curry powders contain garlic powder. Use Keen's

Rissoles in Gravy

Made larger, the meat patties can be used for fantastic burgers.

Prep Time	Cook Time	Total Time	Servings
15 mins	45 mins	1 hour	6

Ingredients

Rissole mixture
500 gm Grade 3 minced beef
Green tops of 2 large leeks, chopped finely
1 medium carrot chopped finely
½ cup flour in which to roll the rissoles
¼ tspn ground Cumin
¼ tspn Ground Coriander
¼ tspn Thyme
1 tblspn GaF Worcestershire Sauce*
1 tblspn Light Soy sauce
2 tspns tomato paste
¾ cup fresh breadcrumbs
Salt and white pepper to taste
1 large egg
Tblspn butter to fry. (Yes,! Butter)

Gravy
1 cup GaF beef stock
Green tops of 3 spring onions
1 tblspn butter
1 tblspn flour
Splash of GaF Worcestershire Sauce

Method
1. Prepare the vegetables
2. Mix flour, spice & thyme in a small bowl. Set aside.
3. Put the meat, veggies, sauces and tomato paste in a large bowl.
4. Mix ingredients together (hands), squeezing the mixture to distribute the meat, onion and carrot evenly.
5. Add the breadcrumbs, salt and pepper. Mix them in throughly.
6. Lightly beat the egg and add it, again mixing well with your hands.
7. The mixture should be moist, not soggy. If it feels too wet, add more breadcrumbs a little at a time until it feels moist but holds together in a ball.
8. Divide the mixture into balls about the size of a pingpong ball.
9. Press each ball between your palms to create a thick patty.
10. Gently toss each rissole in the flour and spices. Shake off the excess.
11. In a frypan heat 1-2 tblspns butter.
12. Fry the rissoles turning them until they are lightly browned all over.
13. Place the fried rissoles in a heat proof rectangular casserole dish, arranging them in rows. (Do not layer them on top of each other. - if the dish is too small to take them all, use 2 dishes.)

Gravy
14. Drop 1 tblspn butter into the frypan and blend it with the meat juices and any pan scrapings.
15. Mix enough flour into the juices to form a thick paste and quickly stir in the beef stock.
16. Keep stirring to make sure the gravy does not go lumpy.
17. Pour the gravy over the rissoles and place in the oven at 180C for 20 minutes, or until the gravy has thickened and the rissoles are fully browned.

Serve with mashed potatoes and a green vegetable.

*See recipe p20

Nanna's Homemade Sausage Rolls

Grandma's recipe - you'll never use sausage mince again.

Prep Time	Cook Time	Total Time	Servings
15 mins (frozen pastry)	50 mins (incl. cooling)	65 mins	Approx 20 rolls

To make a great sausage roll you need a great butcher and high quality puff pastry.

Do not use pre-made sausage mince or sausages.

Find a butcher who is willing to make fresh pork and veal mince for you. If he can't make each type of mince separately, ask him to make a kilo of pork and veal mince that is 50% of each meat and slightly coarse in texture. Order ahead and you should not have a problem. Most old fashioned family butchers are more than happy to provide you with what you want, if you give them notice.

I used to make my own puff pastry, then I discovered Carême frozen pastry. It's hard to find. Pampas frozen puff pastry is fine. I will never make puff pastry again. But then, I'm an old chook and getting a bit lazy!

The secret of a great result is to keep the puff pastry as cool as possible as you work. I don't take it out of the fridge until after I have made the sausage mixture.

Ingredients

1 tbsp olive oil
Green tops of a leek, finely chopped
1 tbsp fennel seeds
500 gm minced pork
500 gm minced veal
40 gm fine breadcrumbs
Large pinch of dried sage
For glazing: egg-wash

Method
The sausage filling
1. Preheat oven to 200C.
2. Heat olive oil in a non-stick frying pan over medium heat,
3. Add leek and fennel seeds, and stir until leek is tender (10-15 minutes).
4. Allow to cool, then transfer to a food processor with the mince and breadcrumbs and pulse to combine.

The pastry
5. Halve the pastry, then use half at a time (keep other half refrigerated) on a lightly floured bench.
6. Form into 18cm x 60cm rectangles with the longest side closest to you.
7. Brush along the opposite edge with egg wash.

Assemble & Cook
8. Place half the mixture along the side closest to you in a log shape.
9. Roll the pastry away from you and over the meat.
10. Seal the pastry edge down.
11. Score top of roll, brush with egg wash, and cut into 5cm portions
12. Place on a tray lined with baking paper.
13. Repeat with rest of pastry and filling.
14. Bake 15 mins. Meanwhile prepare a new pan by placing a wire rack on top of it (not in it!)
15. When the rolls are just golden, quickly transfer them to the wire rack pan
16. Return to the oven and cook further until pastry is golden and crisp (15-20 minutes).

Serve hot with tomato sauce.

Easy Tomato Ketchup

Very yummy with the Sausage Rolls - *contains onion as a main ingredient*

Prep Time	Cook Time	Total Time	Servings
15 mins	60 mins	75 mins	**2 x 350 ml bottles**

Ingredients

450 gm onions
1.5 kg of really ripe tomatoes
175gm sugar
⅔ cup red wine vinegar
1 tspn salt
2 tblspns Keen's mustard powder

Tie these whole spices in a muslin /clean new Chux bag.
½ tspn peppercorns
1 tspn whole allspice
6 cloves

Method

1. Sterlise the bottle
2. Roughly peel and chop the onions and tomatoes.
3. Put all the vegetables in a pan together with the other ingredients and spice bag.
4. Bring to the boil then lower the heat.
5. Simmer uncovered 45 mins, stirring every now and then.
6. Cool slightly.
7. Puree in a blender.
8. Press the puree through a fine sieve.
9. Return to a clean pan.
10. Bring to the boil.
11. Remove from the heat and immediately pour into sterilised, hot bottles and seal.

You can replace the onion with celery or crushed nigella seeds.

Dauphinoise Potatoes

A little bit fancy. Delicious - it's the cream that makes it, so leave it in.

Prep Time	Cook Time	Total Time	Servings
15 mins	1 hr 15 mins	1.5 hrs	4 - 6

For this dish you will need a 1.5L oven proof baking dish, about 18 x 26 cm and 5cm deep.

I have an oval Corningware casserole with a glass lid that is perfect. The glass lid can be used instead of foil, but foil is fine.

The 5 cm depth is important as anything less will be too small and the sauce will overflow, and anything deeper will be too deep and the dish may not cook as well.

Ingredients

1 ½ cups full fat cream
2 tbsp unsalted butter, melted
1.25 kg starchy potatoes (Sebago)
1 tsp salt
¼ tsp white pepper
2 ½ cups gruyere cheese, freshly grated
2 tsp fresh thyme leaves
A little garlic infused olive oil. (Optional)

Serve as a side dish or as a vegetarian meal.

Method
1. Place butter and cream in a jug.
2. Mix until combined.
3. Preheat oven to 180°C
4. Peel the potatoes and slice them 3 mm thick. Or use a mandolin/slicer.
5. *Optional:* Using a piece of paper towel dipped in the garlic infused olive oil, lightly oil the sides and base of your baking dish.
6. Spread ⅓ of the potatoes in the bottom of the dish.
7. Pour over ⅓ of the cream mixture,
8. Scatter with ⅓ of the salt, pepper and thyme.
9. Sprinkle with 3/4 cups cheese.
10. Layers 2 & 3: Repeat for the 2nd and third layer. *Do not use cheese on the top/3rd layer.*
11. Cover with lid or foil
12. Bake for 1 hr 15 min or until the potatoes in the middle are soft.
13. Remove foil, top with cheese.
14. Bake for a further 10 to 15 minutes until golden and bubbly.
15. Stand 5 minutes before serving.

Mediterranean

The Mediterranean Pantry

In around 1950, Mediterranean cuisine became known in the culinary world as the food from that area that bounded the Mediterranean shores and where the olive tree grows naturally - "those blessed lands of sun and sea and olive trees". While this definition has changed over time to encompass more regions and more foods, it remains essentially a cuisine that is rich in oil, bread, wine and fresh vegetables, seafood, fruit and fragrant and aromatic herbs. In this collection I have included some well loved Italian and Greek dishes that would usually contain garlic, but adapted to be garlic free retain their luscious characteristics.

Traditional Mediterranean ingredients

Garlic
While garlic is one of the most popular ingredients, there are many aromatic herbs and yummy ingredients in Italian and Greek food that make it taste fantastic without needing garlic.

However, for those who really want the flavour of garlic, provided it is removed intact prior to adding any other ingredients, you could try a whole garlic clove sautéed in olive oil at the beginning of cooking. ***It has to be removed because the other ingredients would release the fructans into the dish and trigger your symptoms.***

Alternatively, try substituting some FODMAP friendly garlic infused oil for some of the olive oil. Start with a low ratio of garlic infused oil to olive oil, e.g. in a recipe calling for 1/2 cup olive oil, start with a ratio of 1 tblspn of garlic infused oil to 100 ml of olive oil.

Olive oil and Extra virgin olive oil
While olive oil is often used in cooking, extra virgin olive oil is used as a garnish to add a peppery flavour. It is also used as a dip for Italian bread, e.g. focaccia, or drizzled over salad.

Balsamic vinegar.
This dark, well-aged vinegar is used in marinades and dressings.

Fresh tomatoes
The heart of Italian cuisine.

Oregano
Dried oregano leaves add an earthy flavour to marinara sauce, pizza, salad dressing, or grilled meats.

Capers
The pickled flower buds from the Flinders rose bush. These small, salty green orbs are a popular ingredient in Mediterranean dishes like chicken piccata and puttanesca sauce.

Porcini mushrooms
Porcinis, either fresh or dried, are added to sauces, cooked in risotto, or simmered in a wine sauce to add texture to a dish.

Basil
Basil is a fragrant green herb with a smokey, minty taste. It is the most popular herb in Italian cooking. The main ingredient in pesto sauce.

Pasta sauces

- Aglio o Olio - garlic and oil - **Not on the menu for us!!!**
- Marinara - tomatoes, garlic, onion, olive oil, and basil - **remove garlic**
- Pomodoro - same ingredients as marinara but is a thicker, smoother sauce - **remove garlic**
- Bolognese - meat such as ham, beef, and lamb in a tomato and wine sauce
- Pesto - basil, garlic, olive oil, pine nuts, and grated parmesan cheese - **can be made GaF**
- Carbonara - egg yolk, bacon and cheese

Italian & Greek cheese

- Parmigiano-Reggiano, Grana Padano and Kefalotyri - hard cheeses shaved over salads or grated over pasta and soft cheeses like feta and ricotta
- Pecorino - cheese made from sheep's milk.
- Mozzarella - used to melt over meals, like lasagna and pizza.

Pasta.

Pasta is a mix of flour, eggs, olive oil, water, and salt. There are many varieties;

- Acini Di Pepe - extremely small round pasta, like a peppercorn
- Angel Hair - long round very thin pasta
- Casarecce - short lengths of narrow twisted and rolled tube
- Conchigli - shell shaped, several sizes from very large to very small
- Farfalle - bow ties
- Fettuccine - long, flat pasta
- Fusilli - short, twisted spring shape
- Gemelli - unicorn horns
- Gigli - cone or flower shape
- Gnocchi - small oval shapes dough made from potato, eggs, cheese and flour
- Lasagne sheets - flat wide sheets of pasta
- Linguine - similar to fettuccine but much narrower
- Manicotti - huge tube shaped pasta
- Macaroni - small elbow shaped tubes
- Mezzaluna - half moon shaped
- Pappardelle - flat, wide pasta ribbons
- Penne - tube shapes
- Ravioli - pillow shaped pasta stuffed with meat, cheese or vegetable
- Risoni - shaped like rice
- Rotelle - shaped like spoked wheels
- Spaghetti - long, round strands of pasta
- Tagliatelle - thin pasta ribbons
- Tortellini - similar to ravioli but shaped into a ring
- Tortelloni - larger form of Tortellini

Yarithes

The way my friend the chef prepared prawns for me, greek style

Prep Time	Cook Time	Total Time	Servings
15 mins	30 mins	45 mins	4

Ingredients

20 medium uncooked prawns, shelled, tail on and deveined.
6 large egg tomatoes, skinned, de-seeded and roughly chopped.
4 tblspn olive oil
1 tblspn torn fresh basil
2 sprigs of fresh thyme (remove leaves from stalk)
1 tblspn chopped fresh parsley
2 sprigs fresh oregano (remove leaves from stalk)
2 tspns sugar
Freshly ground black pepper
Large pinch salt (to taste)
2 spring onions, slice crossways into 1 cm rounds,
1/2 red capsicum cut into 2 cm cubes
1/4 cup white wine

To serve

4 large Pasta bowls
2 cm cubes of Greek Feta Cheese (or shaved Parmesan if you must)
The leaves from 1 sprig of thyme
1 tblspn chopped parsley
Enough basil leaves (whole) to place 2 on the top of each bowl.

Method

1. Place tomatoes, 2 tblspns olive oil, black pepper, salt and sugar in a medium saucepan over a medium heat.
2. Cook, stirring, until the tomatoes break down into a thick sauce.
3. Taste - if the sauce is a sour/bitter add a touch more sugar.
4. Add the thyme and oregano leaves, basil and parsley.
5. Turn heat to low and simmer until the sauce reduces by ⅓.

Meanwhile;

6. In a fry pan, on a med-high setting, heat 2 tblspns of olive oil.
7. Add the spring onion and capsicum and sauté until soft. Do not brown.
8. Turn up the heat slightly and add the wine, cook 2 mins to evaporate the alcohol.
9. Add the contents of the frypan to the tomato sauce. Bring the sauce to a simmer. It should be thick enough to coat the back of a spoon.
10. Drop in the prawns and simmer gently until the prawns are pink and opaque.

*Place 5 prawns in each pasta bowl.
Pour over the sauce.
Scatter a little fresh thyme and parsley.
Top with several cubes of feta cheese.
Garnish with 2 basil leaves.
Serve immediately
with crusty bread on the side.*

Yarithes

Bolognese Sauce

An old favourite for a family feast

Prep Time	Cook Time	Total Time	Servings
15 mins	2.5 hours	2 hrs 45 mins	6 - 8

Ingredients

2 tblspns Olive oil (or 1½ tblspns olive oil + 2 tspns Garlic infused oil).
Green tops of 5 spring onions chopped
500 gm beef mince (Grade 3 has more fat, therefore more flavour)
A good grind of black pepper (to taste)
½ tspn dried oregano
½ tspn dried basil
½ tspn dried thyme
½ tspn dried rosemary
1 can crushed tomatoes
2 tblspns tomato paste
250 mls GaF Beef Stock. (If using commercial check the ingredients to ensure garlic free).
Salt to taste

To serve ;
60 gms pasta of your choice per person.
Shaved or grated parmesan cheese
Fresh basil leaves to garnish

Recipe Note
While very delicious served straight away, this sauce is always best when left overnight.

Once cool, pop it in the fridge and serve it the following day.

Method

1. Heat the oil in a deep pan .
2. Sauté the onion until translucent.
3. Add the beef mince, stirring to break it up and mix through the onion.
4. Sauté the meat until it starts to brown and separates into small clumps
5. Add crushed tomatoes and tomato paste.
6. Stir to combine well and then add the herbs, stock and pepper.
7. Bring to the boil and then turn the heat down to a simmer.
8. Simmer, uncovered, for an hour or until the sauce has thickened.
9. Turn off and allow to cool.
10. Reheat and keep hot to serve.

Pasta

About 20 mins before you want to serve the meal, cook the pasta.

11. Place at least 3 litres of water in a large pot and bring to a brisk boil.
12. Add 2 tblspns of salt.(It may seem a lot, but the pasta will be really bland without it.)
13. Keep that water boiling and move the pasta around so that it doesn't stick together.
14. When the pasta is al dente (firm but not hard in the centre) strain through a colander and place in a large pasta serving bowl. Mix through ¾ of the sauce and pour the rest over the top.
15. Garnish with basil and serve Parmesan on the side.
16. Allow everyone to serve themselves.

Basil and Pesto Salad

Pasta Salad with garlic free pesto and tomatoes

Prep Time	Cook Time	Total Time	Servings
10 mins	25 mins	35 mins	6

Ingredients

500 gms Farfalle (Bow-Tie pasta) uncooked
350 gms fresh green beans stems removed
1½ cup cherry tomatoes halved lengthwise and seeded
¾ cup chopped, fresh Mozzarella
¾ cup GaF Basil Pesto*
Generous pinch of salt

Method

1. Have ready a large pot of heavily salted water and bring to a boil over high heat.
2. Add pasta and cook to 'al dente' according to package instructions.
3. Strain over the sink and rinse with a stream of cool water to avoid overcooking. Set aside until ready to use.
4. For the green beans, add water to a medium-sized saucepan until about two-thirds of the way full.
5. Place over high heat and bring to a boil. Add green beans to water and allow to boil for 6 minutes, just until tender.
6. Remove from the heat, strain and rinse, once again, with a stream of cool running water to avoid further cooking.
7. Transfer pasta and green beans to a large mixing bowl, along with the tomatoes, Mozzarella, pesto and salt.
8. Gently fold ingredients together.
9. Serve right away or refrigerate for up to 3 days.

* See Section - Basics for GaF Pesto recipe

Mushroom & Thyme Linguine

*To make this a vegetarian dish use Bio-Parmesan**

Prep Time	Cook Time	Total Time	Servings
15 mins	20 mins	35 mins	6

Ingredients

225 gms button mushrooms
80 mls extra virgin olive oil
Tspn salt
Juice and zest of 1 lemon
4 sprigs fresh thyme (stripped from sprig)
500 grams linguine
1 bunch fresh parsley (chopped)
3 tablespoons freshly grated parmesan cheese (or to taste)
Freshly ground black pepper to taste

Instructions

1. Finely slice the mushrooms.
2. Put them in a large bowl with the oil, salt, lemon juice and zest, and thyme leaves.
3. Cook the pasta according to packet instructions and drain.
4. Put the drained pasta into the bowl with the mushroom mixture.
5. Toss everything together well
6. Add the chopped parsley, grated cheese and pepper to taste.
7. Toss again and serve immediately.

Available from Woolworths

Leek & Mushroom Risotto

Luscious and fragrant with thyme

Prep Time	Cook Time	Total Time	Servings
15 mins	40 mins	55 mins	4

Ingredients

25 gm dried mushroom pieces
1.5 litres hot garlic free chicken/vegetable stock *
120 gm butter, diced
40 ml olive oil
500 gm fresh assorted mushrooms, (any kind but mix them up) thickly sliced.
1 leek (white and pale green parts only), halved and thinly sliced
400 gm arborio rice
1 tbsp fresh thyme leaves stripped from the sprigs (or use dried thyme)
125 ml dry white wine
120 gm marscapone cheese
50 gm fresh parmesan, finely grated, plus extra to serve
Finely grated rind of 1 lemon

Method

1. Soak dried mushroom pieces in 250ml hot stock in a bowl until soft (8-10 minutes), then pour into remaining stock.
2. While the mushrooms are soaking, put the rice in a large sieve and rinse thoroughly in cold water to remove the starch.
3. Heat 20ml olive oil and 30gm butter in a large frying pan over medium-high heat until butter foams, add fresh mushrooms and fry until tender and golden brown (2-3 minutes)
4. Heat remaining olive oil and 50gm butter in a wide saucepan over medium heat until it starts to foam.
5. Add leek and sauté until translucent (5-6 minutes).
6. Stir in rice and thyme to coat in oil and lightly toast, then add wine and stir until almost evaporated (1-2 minutes).
7. Add hot stock a ladleful at a time, stirring continuously until stock is absorbed before adding the next, until rice is al dente (15-18 minutes - you may not need all the stock).
8. Season to taste, stir in mascarpone, parmesan, lemon rind, remaining butter and two-thirds of the flat mushrooms.
9. Serve topped with remaining mushrooms and extra parmesan.

*See Garlic Free Basics Section for GaF stock

Pumpkin & Goat's Cheese Lasagne

Vegetarian lasagne that everyone will love

Prep Time	Cook Time	Total Time	Servings
15mins	2 hrs 45 mins	3 hours	6

Ingredients

For the Pumpkin layer

Half a Jap pumpkin.
20 ml olive oil
20 grams butter
8 sage leaves
4 large spring onions, green tops only, finely chopped
50 mls white wine
40 mls water
400 gm tin chopped tomatoes
salt & pepper

For the Tomato Sauce

1 bottle passata
500 ml water
2 x tablespoons sugar
1 tablespoon table salt
Freshly ground black pepper to taste salt & pepper

For the Cheese layer

450 grams soft goat's cheese
500 grams ricotta cheese
3 eggs
Freshly ground nutmeg (be generous)
600 grams fresh lasagne sheets
2 balls of mozzarella

Method

1. Peel and deseed the pumpkin. Cut into small cubes (2-3 cm).
2. Heat the oil and butter in a shallow deep frying pan.
3. Gently fry the sage leaves for about 2 minutes.
4. Add the chopped spring onion to the pan and fry very gently for another 10 minutes.
5. Add the pumpkin pieces, cook 5 minutes, stirring gently.
6. Add the wine, water and chopped tomatoes.
7. Simmer, covered, for an hour, stirring occasionally so the pumpkin cooks evenly.
8. Add seasoning to taste.
9. Leave to cool.
10. Pour the passata and water into a large jug.
11. Stir in the sugar, salt and pepper, whisking well.
12. In a separate bowl beat the goat's cheese and ricotta with the eggs, nutmeg, and salt and pepper to taste.
13. Preheat the oven to 200°C.
14. Put 500ml tomato sauce in the bottom of a roasting tin.
15. Put the remaining tomato sauce aside.

Cooking & Eating in a Garlic-Free Zone

To assemble

16. Create a layer with a third of the lasagne sheets, overlapping them well.
17. Spoon over a third of the cheese mixture in dollops, and spread each one out with a spatula.
18. Repeat twice - a layer of lasagne, followed by pumpkin, then the cheese.
19. Pour the remaining cold tomato sauce over the lasagne, letting it sink down and be absorbed in the layers.
20. Slice and chop the mozzarella balls and dot over the top. Cook in the oven, on the baking sheet, for 1 hour.
21. Once cooked, take out of the oven and let it stand for at least 15 - 30 minutes.
22. Sprinkle the toasted pine nuts over the lasagne, and cut into squares to serve.

Minestrone my way

Cheesy and hearty and oh so yummy!

Prep Time	Cook Time	Total Time	Servings
25 mins	35 mins	60 mins	8

Ingredients

60 ml extra-virgin olive oil, plus extra to serve
250 gms chuck steak, sinew removed and cut into 1cm cubes
2 leeks, finely chopped
1 bulb fennel finely chopped
1 celery heart sliced
2 fresh bay leaves
350 gm waxy potatoes, such as Nicola, cut into 1cm dice
½ tin borlotti, cannellini or similar beans
200 gm tinned crushed tomatoes, crushed
½ cup carnaroli/arborio rice
1 L GaF beef stock *
½ litre cold water
1 cup (loosely packed) flat-leaf parsley, coarsely chopped
60 gms parmesan cheese cut in 1 cm chunks
Freshly grated parmesan and crusty bread, to serve

To serve, scatter with plenty of parmesan, drizzle with olive oil and serve with crusty bread.

Method

1. Heat olive oil in a large saucepan over medium-high heat.
2. Add beef and stir until the cubes are sealed, but not browned.
3. Add leeks, celery and bay leaves
4. Sauté vegetables without colouring, until softened (3-5 minutes).
5. Add potato, beans and tomato.
6. Add the cold water, if necessary add more until ingredients are covered.
7. Bring to the boil over high heat, add rice, season to taste and stir to combine.
8. Reduce heat to medium and simmer 30 mins.
9. Add the rice and bring back to the simmer.
10. Simmer until beef and rice are cooked and tender.
11. Add parsley and parmesan cubes and simmer until parmesan starts to soften (5 minutes).
12. Season to taste.

• *See Basics Section for GaF Beef Stock recipe*

Chicken Cacciatore

If you like garlic, try using Cobram's garlic infused oil

Prep Time	Cook Time	Total Time	Servings
15 mins	40 mins	55 mins	4

Ingredients

1 x 15ml tablespoon Cobram's garlic infused olive oil (FODMAP labelled)
6 spring onions (finely sliced)
75 grams bacon (cut into cubes)
Green tops of 6 spring onions (finely sliced)
1 teaspoon rosemary (strip from stalk and finely chop leaves)
500 grams chicken thigh fillets quartered
1 teaspoon celery salt*
125 mls white wine
1 can chopped skinless tomatoes
2 bay leaves
1 teaspoon sugar
1 can cannellini beans, drained.

Method

1. Heat the oil in a heavy-based pan and fry the bacon cubes, sliced spring onions and chopped rosemary, stirring for 2-3 minutes.
2. Add chicken pieces, stir well to coat and lightly brown.
3. Add celery salt.
4. Pour in the wine allow come to a simmer before adding the tomatoes, bay leaves and sugar.
5. Cover and allow to simmer for 15-20 minutes.
6. Add Cannellini beans.
7. Bring back to the simmer until beans are hot.
8. Serve with crusty bread.

*Check celery salt ingredients, some brands contain garlic.

Moussaka

The Greek version of lasagne, made with eggplant, not pasta

Prep Time	Cook Time	Total Time	Servings
45 mins	2hrs	2 hrs 45 mins	6-8

Ingredients

6 eggplants - stalks removed cut into 1cm slices, vegetable oil

For meat sauce
750g beef or lamb mince
Green tops of 2 large leeks (chopped)
1 x 400gm tin chopped skinless tomatoes
2 tbsp tomato paste
1 teaspoon sugar
1 glass of red wine
Pinch of sea salt and freshly ground black pepper
1 bay leaf
A pinch of cinnamon or one cinnamon stick
¼ of a cup olive oil (use Garlic infused oil if you wish the garlic flavour)

Potato - Optional
Sometimes moussaka is made with a layer of sliced potato as the base.
5 potatoes peeled and sliced into 2cm thick rounds.

For Béchamel Sauce
900ml milk
120g butter
120g flour
Pinch of nutmeg
2 egg yolks
100g Parmigiano-Reggiano or Kefalotyri
Salt to taste

Method

Prepare the eggplants.
1. Season with salt and place in a colander for 30 mins.
2. Rinse with plenty of water and squeeze to get rid of excess water.
3. Pat dry and fry in plenty of oil, until nicely coloured.
4. Place the fried eggplants on paper towel to absorb the oil.
5. Set aside when done

Note: for a healthier dish, bake the eggplant in the oven at 180C until starts to brown.

Meat Sauce.
6. Heat a large pan to med-high and add the olive oil.
7. Stir in the chopped leeks and sauté, until softened and slightly colored.
8. Stir in the mince breaking it up with a wooden spoon and sauté.
9. When brown, add tomato paste and sauté a few minutes longer.
10. Pour in the red wine and wait for alcohol to evaporate.
11. Add tomatoes, sugar, pinch of cinnamon, 1 bay leaf and a good pinch of salt and pepper.
12. Bring to the boil, turn the heat down simmer, lid on, for 30 mins or until most of the juices have evaporated.
13. Set aside when done.

Potatoes - Optional
14. Fry / bake until brown on both sides (flip over when first side is brown).

Cooking & Eating in a Garlic-Free Zone

Béchamel Sauce

15. In a large pan, melt butter over low-medium heat.
16. Add the flour whisking continuously to make a paste.
17. Add warmed milk in a steady stream; keep whisking in order to prevent your sauce from getting lumpy.
18. If the sauce still needs to thicken, boil over low heat while continuing to stir. Its consistency should resemble a thick cream.
19. Remove the béchamel pan from the stove and stir in the egg yolks, salt, pepper, a pinch of nutmeg and the most of the grated cheese. Reserve some cheese to sprinkle on top!
20. Whisk quickly, in order to prevent the eggs from turning an omelette!
21. Season with salt to taste.
22. Take one spoon full of béchamel and stir it in the meat sauce.
23. Set the béchamel sauce aside.

Assemble and cook the Moussaka

24. For this moussaka recipe you will need a large baking dish, approx. 20x30cm / and 8cm deep.
25. Butter the bottom and sides of the pan (Optional - lay down a layer of potato).
26. Put down a layer of half the eggplant.
27. Pour in all of the meat sauce and spread it out evenly.
28. Add a second layer of eggplant.
29. Top with all of the béchamel sauce and smooth out with a spatula.
30. Sprinkle with the remaining grated cheese.
31. Preheat your oven to 180C/350F and bake for about 60 minutes or until its crust turns light golden brown.

Veal and Mushroom Pasta

*Substitute veal for beef in our garlic free beef stock**

Prep Time	Cook Time	Total Time	Servings
10 mins	20 mins	30 mins	4

Ingredients

500 gm assorted mushrooms,
e.g. Swiss brown, Portobello, oyster, button.
30 gm butter, coarsely chopped
1 tbsp olive oil
1 tsp finely chopped rosemary leaves
80 ml dry white wine
375 ml veal or vegetable stock
1 cup coarsely torn flat-leaf-parsley leaves, plus extra to serve
400 gm fresh pappardelle

Method

1. Chop large mushrooms into chunks, combine in a bowl with remaining mushrooms.
2. Heat butter and olive oil in a casserole over high heat until foaming.
3. Add mushrooms and rosemary, stir occasionally until golden (2-4 mins).
4. Add wine, cook until reduced by two-thirds (1-2 mins)
5. Add stock and cook until reduced by half (5-10 mins).
6. Stir through parsley, season and keep warm.
7. Meanwhile, cook pasta in a large saucepan of boiling salted water until 'al dente' (time varies, check on the packet).
8. Drain and divide among bowls.
9. Spoon over sauce and serve immediately drizzled with extra-virgin olive oil and scattered with extra parsley and parmesan.

* See Basics Section recipe

Roast Chicken Italian Style

*For garlic flavour swap some of the olive oil with garlic infused oil**

Prep Time	Cook Time	Total Time	Servings
15 mins	60 mins	75 mins	6

Ingredients

1.5 kg fresh whole chicken
1 lemon
6 sticks fresh rosemary (10-15cm long)
3 leeks
2 red & 2 green capsicum
100 grams pitted black olives
60 mls olive oil (or optionally - 50mls olive oil and 10mls garlic infused oil mixed together)
salt & black pepper to taste

Method

1. Preheat the oven to 200°C/180°C
2. Place chicken in a roasting tin
3. Halve the lemon and put the halves and 2 sprigs of rosemary into the cavity.
4. Chop each leek into 3 pieces, slice lengthways and place in a large bowl.
5. Core and de-seed the capsicums, slice them into strips and add to the bowl.
6. Scatter the olives over the vegetable.
7. Pour ⅔ of the olive oil over all.
8. Sprinkle the salt and pepper around to taste
9. Gently toss the vegetables to help coat them with the oil and ensure they are well mixed.
10. Pour the remaining ⅓ of the oil over the chicken and sprinkle some sea salt flakes over it.
11. Spread the vegetables evenly around the chicken.
12. Poke the remaining rosemary sprigs into the middle of the vegetables at even spaces.
13. Place the roasting tin in the oven and cook 60 - 90 mins
14. Check that the chicken is cooked through. (The juices should be clear when you slip a knife into the thickest part of the thigh joint).
15. Remove the chicken and place onto a carving board
16. Turn off the oven and put the pan of vegetables back into the oven until you are ready to serve, together with a large serving platter (to warm).
17. Rest the chicken for 10 mins.
18. When rested cut the chicken into pieces.
19. Remove the warm platter and the roasting tin from the oven.
20. With a slotted spoon, lift the vegetables from the roasting pan and spread them over the warm platter.
21. Arrange the chicken pieces on top of the vegetables.
22. Pour the pan juices over the chicken and vegetables.
23. Serve to the table immediately.

See the Basics Section for home made or bought Garlic Infused Oil.

Lamb Souvlaki

Cook the lamb well, it should not be pink!! GaF & OF

Prep Time	Cook Time	Total Time	Servings
6 hrs 15 mins incl marinating	20 mins	6hrs 20 mins	4

Ingredients

1kg lamb leg or shoulder, cut into 3 cm chunks
½ cup olive oil (optional Garlic Infused Oil for the garlic lovers)
juice of 1 lemon
tsp ground Nigella seeds
1 tsp dried oregano
1 tsp dried thyme or some fresh thyme, chopped
½ tsp smoked paprika
½ tsp cumin
salt and freshly ground pepper
8 metal or wooden skewers

Tzatziki

1 cucumber
1 teaspoon Garlic infused Olive Oil (optional)
¼ of a cup extra virgin olive oil
500g of Greek yoghurt
1–2 tbsps of red wine vinegar
a pinch of salt

To serve

8 pita breads
olive oil
1 tsp dried oregano
salt
Tzatziki
Greek salad

Method

Marinate the lamb

1. In a large bowl add the olive oil, lemon juice, the herbs and spices and season with freshly ground pepper.
2. Whisk all the ingredients to combine.
3. Add the meat and mix to coat.
4. Cover the bowl with plastic wrap, chill and let marinate for at least 6 hours, or better still, overnight. Stir every now and again to make sure all the lamb is marinated well.

Assemble & cook the souvlaki

5. To assemble the lamb kebab you can either use wooden or metal skewers. If using wooden skewers, cut them to fit your grill and soak them in water. to stop them burning.
6. Lift the chunks of lamb out of the marinade and thread the pieces on the skewers. Season your lamb souvlaki with salt.
7. Heat a grill, barbecue or griddle pan
8. Cook the lamb kebab for about 10-15 minutes, until cooked to your liking.

Pita breads.

9. Preheat the oven to 220C.
10. Use a pastry brush to oil the pita breads on both sides
11. Season with salt and oregano.
12. Place the pita breads on top of a large oven tray at the bottom of the oven Bake for 2-3 minutes. Or toast on both sides.

Cooking & Eating in a Garlic-Free Zone

Tzatziki

1. Remove the skin and the seeds of the cucumber and grate it into a large bowl.
2. Season with salt and pepper and leave aside for 10 minutes.
3. Wrap the grated cucumber in a towel and squeeze, to remove excess water.
4. In a bowl, add the cucumber, oil, yoghurt, red wine vinegar, a pinch of salt
5. Blend, until the ingredients are combined.
6. Store the tzatziki sauce in the fridge and always serve cold.

Recipe Note

Souvlaki is a popular and very delicious street food.

Traditionally, the meat is removed from the skewer placed on the pita and smothered with wonderful tzatziki before being wrapped in the bread and eaten as you stroll along .

Served on a long platter, with a fresh greek salad and tzatziki on the side, it's equally at home as a great barbecue dish for friends and family to celebrate on any occasion.

This recipe is both garlic and onion free. The Nigella adds the onion flavour.

For those who like garlic, but can't eat it, substituting some of the olive oil in the marinade with garlic free oil will give them their garlic hit!

Keftedes

Juicy, crunchy little bites of heaven!! GaF and OF

Prep Time	Cook Time	Total Time	Servings
60 mins	30 mins	1.5 hours	About 40 meatballs

Ingredients

500g beef mince
200g pork mince
1 tsp ground nigella seeds
150g stale bread soaked in water and squeezed to remove the excess water
1 large egg
1½ tbsp fresh flat leaf parsley, chopped
1½ tbsp fresh mint (chopped) and a pinch dried mint
2 tbsps olive oil
(or 1 tblspn Garlic infused olive oil and 1 tblspn olive oil)
1½ tbsps red wine vinegar
1 teaspoon oregano
1 teaspoon salt
1 teaspoon pepper
oil for frying
flour for dredging

Method

1. Add all the ingredients into a large bowl.
2. Mix well, squeezing to blend the flavours.
3. Cover the bowl with plastic wrap.
4. Place in the fridge for 1 hour.
5. Turn the mixture for the keftedes out of the fridge.
6. Roll into meatballs the size of a walnut.
7. Dredge the rolled meatballs lightly in flour - shake off any excess.
8. Fry the keftedes in batches of 10-15 at a time, until nicely browned on all sides.

Recipe note

Serve as an appetizer with tzatziki sauce and pita breads or as a main course with basmati rice and a Greek salad.

OR - eat them with pasta and a tangy tomato sugo as a mixture of Greek and Italian cuisine.

Greek Salad

I love my Greek Salad - GaF (contains onion but you can leave it out)

Prep Time	Cook Time	Total Time	Servings
15 mins	5 mins	20 mins	4

Ingredients

1 Lebanese cucumber, cut lengthwise, seeded, and sliced 5cm thick
3 medium tomatoes quartered
200 gms feta cheese, cut into 1 cm cubes
⅓ cup thinly sliced red onion
⅓ cup pitted Kalamata olives
Fresh oregano (pick the leaves from the stalk)

Note: The recipe for the dressing for this salad is below.

Method

To assemble the salad:-

1. On a large shallow bowl, arrange the cucumber, tomatoes, feta cheese, red onions, and olives.
2. Drizzle with the dressing and gently toss.
3. Sprinkle with a few generous pinches of oregano.
4. Season to taste and serve.

Lemon, Basil and Oil Marinade/Dressing

The perfect dressing for Greek/Italian Salad/any salad really

Prep Time	Cook Time	Total Time	Servings
5 mins	N/A	5 mins	N/A

Ingredients

1 Lemon
½ tbsp. of balsamic vinegar,
½ tspn extra Olive oil **or**
½ tspn garlic-infused oil (optional)
1 tbsp. of chopped fresh basil

You can replace the onion with celery or crushed nigella seeds.

Method

1. Juice the lemon
2. Combine all the ingredients in a small jug.
3. Pour over char-grilled vegetables such as zucchini, capsicum and eggplant.

The Indian Pantry

I first tasted home-cooked Indian food in Fiji. To my surprise, I found that my impression of Indian food as being hot, hot, hot with chili was wrong. The amount of chili is a matter of personal choice, and flavour bursts from every mouthful.

When asked if I would like to learn how to cook Indian food, I jumped at the opportunity. I learnt to include 6 -7 cloves of garlic in almost every dish, and loved it. When I became garlic intolerant, it came as a dreadful blow. Later, I found groups who did not eat garlic for religious and cultural reasons. They included Asifoetida instead. It became my go-to substitute for garlic, but I don't always use it. I have found there are so many spices that give Indian food its wonderful flavour and warmth, that garlic and chili are not really missed. Garlic free Indian food is always absolutely delicious.

Your Indian pantry should include;

Dry goods
Curry Leaves

Curry powder - a good curry powder has the basic spices already ground and does not contain garlic. I use Keen's Curry Powder, ('Clive of India' contains garlic granules).

Dals (dried pulses) - Lentils, peas and beans

Jaggery (Palm Sugar)

Coconut - Grated, oil, milk and flaked

Tamarind

Amchur (dried mango powder)

Cardamom Pods

Vegetables
Potato, Onion, Tomato, Cauliflower, Cabbage, Bean, Egg Plants, Cucumber and Gherkin, Frozen Peas, Garlic and okra.

Dairy
Ghee (clarified butter), butter, paneer (Indian cheese), milk, yoghurt

Spices
If you keep these spices in your pantry, and freshly grind them or use unground whole spices, you will always be able to enjoy great food!!

cinnamon quills	garam masala
star anise	bay leaves
yellow mustard seed	nigella seeds
black mustard seed	ground anise
fenugreek	ground cardamom
asifoetida	ground coriander
black mustard seed	cayenne pepper
yellow mustard seed	cardamom pods

Indian Cottage Pie

Indian Cottage Pie

A new take on mother's speciality!

Prep Time	Cook Time	Total Time	Servings
15 mins	45 mins	1 hr	6

Ingredients

For the filling
500 grams minced beef/lamb
4 cm piece fresh root ginger, peeled
Tops of three spring onions
½ tspn cardamom seeds
1 tspns ground cumin
1 tspns ground coriander seeds
2 tblspns coconut oil
2 tspns garam masala
¼ tspn Cayenne pepper
1 tspn ground turmeric
1 x 400g tin chopped tomatoes
100 gms red lentils
1 tspn salt flakes
2 x tblspns Worcestershire sauce

For the topping
1 kg sweet potato
2 tspns salt flakes
2 x 15ml tblspns white peppercorns
½ tspn ground cardamom
Peel strips and the juice of 1 lime
About 1 litre cold water
4 cm piece fresh root ginger, peeled and grated*

Method

Preheat your oven to 220C or 180C FF

1. Peel & cut sweet potato into 4-5cm chunks
2. Put the potato chunks into a large saucepan.
3. Add the salt, peppercorns, cardamom and lime strips.
4. Cover the potato with cold water, bring to the boil, put the lid on and simmer 30 minutes - or until tender.

While the potato is cooking

1. Slice the ginger, quarter the spring onion, and put them into a food processor with the cardamom, cumin and coriander. Pulse until finely chopped.
2. Heat the coconut oil in a heavy-based pan and then add the spice paste.
3. Cook until softened stirring, then stir in the garam masala and turmeric.
4. Add the mince, stirring to break it up.
5. Add the chopped tomatoes, then add one tin of cold water.
6. Stir in the red lentils.
7. Add salt and Worcestershire sauce.
8. Bring to a simmer, put on the lid, lower the heat and cook about 25 mins, stirring frequently.
9. When the sweet potatoes are cooked, drain them, reserving the liquid.
10. Put the flesh into a bowl and mash.
11. Slowly beat in some of the potato cooking water until you have a nice mash consistency, and squeeze in the juice of half the lime.
12. Spoon the grated ginger into the centre of a piece of clean Chux. Pull up the edges of the Chux and twist them, into a bag around the ginger.
13. Squeeze and wring out the ginger juice over the mash. Beat it in.
14. Check the seasoning.
15. Once the filling is cooked, ladle it into a large rectangular dish, approx. 30 x 20 x 5cm deep. Top with the mash.
16. Sit the dish on an oven tray and place in the oven for 20 mins or until the mash is piping hot.

* Grate at the last minute as you will be using only the squeezed ginger juice.

Alu Gobi

Popular potato and cauliflower curry

Prep Time	Cook Time	Total Time	Servings
15 mins	20 mins	35 mins	4

Ingredients

2 tbsp. vegetable oil
1 red chilli, diced
1 tbsp. minced ginger
1 tsp. garam masala
½ tsp. dried turmeric
¼ tsp. cayenne pepper
3 floury potatoes peeled and chopped into 2cm pieces
1 medium head cauliflower, cut into florets
1 cup low salt, GaF vegetable stock
Salt
Pinch Asafoetida
Freshly ground black pepper
Freshly chopped Coriander/Parsley, for serving

Method

1. Heat the oil in a large skillet over medium-high heat.
2. Add chilli, asafoetida and ginger and cook until fragrant, 1 minute.
3. Add garam masala, turmeric, and cayenne and cook until toasted. (1 minute more.)
4. Add potatoes, cauliflower, and vegetable stock and season with salt and pepper.
5. Reduce heat and cook, covered, until potatoes and cauliflower are tender, 15 mins.
6. Garnish with coriander to serve.

Alu Gosht

Meat and Potato curry - no heat, no garlic, and very tasty

Prep Time	Cook Time	Total Time	Servings
30 mins	70 mins	1.5 hrs	4

If you want a little heat to this dish, a long green chili (banana chili), seeds removed and coarsely chopped, added to the tomatoes in the third bowl, will give you the bite you are looking for!

Ingredients

1 kg boneless lamb/beef/chicken, cubed
1lb potatoes, peeled and cubed
1 cup beef stock
1 large leek finely chopped
2 inches fresh ginger root
2 tsp Turmeric
1 tsp ground Coriander
1 tsp ground Cumin
1 tsp ground black pepper
6 cloves
6 cardamom pods
2 tomatoes coarsely chopped
3 tsp Garam Masala
1 tsp salt

Method

You will need 3 bowls and a large heavy based saucepan.

Preparation

1. Cube the potatoes and meat and put to one side in separate containers.
2. Take bowl 1. Place the leek, and the ginger in this bowl.
3. In bowl 2, place turmeric, coriander, cumin, black pepper, cloves and cardamom pods.
4. Place the tomatoes, in bowl 3 together with the Garam Masala and salt.

Cooking

5. Heat enough oil to coat the bottom of a large pan then add the contents of bowl 1 and cook 3-4 minutes, until the leek is starting to brown.
6. Add the spices and stir to coat the leek, cooking another 1-2 mins.
7. Add the meat, stir to brown it.
8. Pour in stock and bring to a boil. Reduce heat, cover, and simmer 30 mins.
9. Add the potatoes and stir well. Cover and simmer another 15-20 mins, until the potatoes are tender.
10. Add bowl 3 and stir well. Leave uncovered and simmer another 5-10 minutes.

Serve as a vegetarian dish, or as an accompaniment to meat based main.

Chicken Biryani

This stove-top version is a great favourite with my family

Prep Time	Cook Time	Total Time	Servings
30 mins	1 hour	1.5 hours	6

Ingredients
2 teaspoons ginger paste divided
1 teaspoon turmeric powder
1 tspn ground cardamom
¼ cup plain yogurt
1 teaspoon vegetable oil
1 kg bone-in chicken pieces
1 tablespoon ghee or unsalted butter
⅓ cup finely chopped leek(about ½ of a large leek)

For the rice:
2 cups long grain basmati rice
3 to 4 whole black cardamom pods
3 to 4 whole green cardamom pods
1 cm cinnamon stick
1 teaspoon whole peppercorns
1 to 2 bay leaves
Salt to taste

For the saffron milk:
½ teaspoon saffron threads
⅓ cup cold milk

For the fried onions:
1 cup cooking oil
1 cup thinly sliced leek(about ½ of a large leek)

For assembling the biryani:
1 teaspoon ghee (clarified butter) or unsalted butter
¼ cup coriander, coarsely chopped
¼ cup mint, coarsely chopped
¼ cup plain yogurt
1 ½ teaspoons garam masala
2 to 3 tablespoons pomegranate seeds

Method
Rinse the rice:
1. In a bowl of water, swirl the rice with your hands several times. Tip the rice into a fine-mesh strainer.
2. Repeat rinsing until clear.
3. When clear strain through a fine colander or sieve.

Make the saffron milk
4. Stir the saffron strands into the milk. Cover and set aside for 30 minutes or until ready to layer the biryani.

Prepare and cook the chicken:
5. Cut each thigh in half along the bone; the pieces will be uneven in size with the bone in one half.
6. Sprinkle the chicken all over with salt and pepper.
7. Sear the chicken.
8. Heat the oil on a medium heat in a heavy pot heat the oil.
9. When it is hot, add the chicken, skin side down.
10. Cook for 5 minutes without disturbing.
11. Turn the chicken and cook the other side for 4 minutes.
12. Transfer to a bowl.
13. Discard all but 2 tblspns fat from the pan.

Cook the onion and spices:
14. Add the leek and ginger to the pot and turn the heat to medium-low.
15. Cook, stirring often, for 8 minutes, or until they soften.
16. Add the turmeric and cardamom.
17. Cook, stirring, for 1 minute more.

Cooking & Eating in a Garlic-Free Zone

Add the rice and seared chicken:
18. Add the rice to the pan and stir it into the leek and spices.
19. Return the seared chicken to the pan, along with any juices that have accumulated in the bowl.
20. Turn the chicken in the spices so the pieces are coated all over.
21. Add the cinnamon, bay leaf, raisins, and water.
22. Pour the saffron milk over the dish.

Cook the biryani:
23. Bring the water to a boil, then lower the heat and cover the pan.
24. Simmer for 18 minutes, or until the rice is tender and the chicken is cooked through.
25. Remove the pan from the heat; set aside for 5 minutes.

Toast the almonds:
26. In a dry skillet over medium heat, toast the almonds, shaking the pan often, for 5 minutes. Chop coarsely.

Plate the biryani:
27. Remove the bay leaf and cinnamon stick from the rice.
28. Taste and add additional salt, pepper, or cardamom to suit your taste.
29. Sprinkle the dish with almonds, pomegranate seeds and fresh coriander.

Serve and enjoy!!!

Naan Bread

Doesn't have to be garlic - add any flavour you fancy

Prep Time	Cook Time	Total Time	Servings
4 hours - inc rising	5 minutes per naan	4.5 hours	**6 naan**

Ingredients

1 cup lukewarm milk
1½ teaspoons active dry yeast
2 teaspoons sugar
4 cups plain flour + extra for dusting
Tspn nigella seeds (adds oniony flavour)
2 teaspoons salt
2 tablespoons vegetable or canola oil + extra for greasing the bowl
½ cup plain yogurt

Suggestions

If you like flavoured Naan, you can add such spices and flavours as;

Nigella seeds for an oniony flavour
Garam Masala for a mild Indian curry flavour
If you like garlic add a little garlic infused oil instead of canola oil
Ground anise for a licorice flavour
Poppy seeds
Sesame seeds

Add any spices or flavours to the flour before you mix in the yoghurt and milk and yeast mixture.

Prepare a bowl:

Lightly grease a large bowl with a little bit of oil. Set the bowl aside. (You will put your dough in this bowl to let it rise.)

Method
Prepare the dough:

1. In a liquid measuring cup or a small mixing bowl, combine the lukewarm milk, sugar, and active dry yeast, (just warm to the touch. If it's too hot you can kill the yeast).
2. Let it sit for 5 minutes.
3. In another large mixing bowl, whisk the flour and salt any spices.
4. Add yogurt, oil and milk-yeast mixture. Use a wooden spoon or your hands to combine the dough.
5. The dough should be soft and sticky at this point.

Knead the dough:

6. Dust your kitchen bench top with flour.
7. Transfer the dough to the bench top.
8. Knead together until a soft dough forms, about 5 minutes. If it feels dry and is hard to knead, add 1-2 tblspns of water, a little bit at a time, until the dough is easier to work with.

Let the dough rise:

9. Transfer the dough to the greased bowl.
10. Cover the bowl with plastic wrap or a damp towel.
11. Place in a dark, warm, dry place.
12. Let the dough rise for 3-4 hours or until it more than doubles in size.
13. Let the dough rise for 3-4 hours or until it more than doubles in size.

Cooking & Eating in a Garlic-Free Zone

To cook the Naan

14. Fill a small bowl with flour. Dust some of the flour onto a work surface.
15. Turn out the dough, dust with flour.
16. Shape the dough into a rectangle, adding more flour as necessary so it doesn't stick.
17. Divide into six equal portions.
18. Heat a cast iron or heavy nonstick pan over med-high heat until very hot.
19. While it heats, roll one of the dough balls into a rectangle about ½ cm thick.
20. Place the dough in the hot, dry skillet and cook until the surface is full of air bubbles and the bottom is browned and blistered in spots.
21. Flip the naan and cook a few minutes more.
22. Brush the cooked naan with melted butter, and cook remaining balls.
23. Sprinkle with parsley, if using, then serve warm.

Why not experiment and see what flavours you can bring to your Naan?

Chicken Korma

Yummy, yummy, yummy!! However, contains onion.

Prep Time	Cook Time	Total Time	Servings
20 mins + marinating	1 hr 10 mins	1.5 hours + marinating	6

Ingredients

For the sauce:

12 to 15 raw almonds
2 to 3 green cardamom pods
1/2 teaspoon freshly cracked peppercorn
1-inch cinnamon stick
2 to 3 whole cloves
1 bay leaf
1 tablespoon ground coriander
1/2 teaspoon salt or to taste
1/4 cup plain yogurt
1 1/2 teaspoon shredded coconut, optional
Silvered almonds and chopped cilantro, for garnish

For the marinade:

2 kgs boneless chicken thighs, cut into 2 cm thick pieces
2 tablespoons plain yogurt
½ teaspoon ground turmeric
1½ tablespoons ginger paste
½ teaspoon salt
1 teaspoon cayenne pepper

For the onions:

1 medium onion, thinly sliced, about 1 cup
½ cup vegetable oil

Optional - replace the onion with cup of finely slicd celery and teaspoon crushed nigella seeds.

Method

Marinate the chicken:

1. In a medium-sized mixing bowl combine yogurt, turmeric, ginger paste, salt, and cayenne pepper.
2. Using a spoon or a whisk, mix it all together.
3. Add chicken to the marinade. Coat the chicken well . Cover with a plate and set aside in the refrigerator for 1 hour.

Make the almond paste:

4. Soak the almonds in 1/2 cup water for approximately 2 hours, then peel .
5. In a blender /grinder grind the almonds into a smooth paste. If necessary, add 1-2 tblspns of water to help with a smooth grinding.

Fry the Onions (or celery)

6. Heat oil in a Dutch oven over medium-high heat.
7. Line a plate or sheet pan with paper towels and set this near the stove.
8. Check to see if the oil is hot enough by dropping a strand of onion into the pot. If it sizzles then the oil is ready.
9. Add the rest of the onions to the pot.
10. Cook for 7-10 minutes on medium-high heat, stirring, until the onions turn golden brown.
11. Use a slotted spoon to take the onions out of the oil and spread into the paper-towel to soak up the excess oil.
12. Set aside for later. You will use these onions to make a paste.
13. Leave about 1 tablespoon of oil in the pot and discard the rest.

You can replace the onion with celeryand crushed nigella seeds.

Start cooking the chicken:

14. Add cardamom, peppercorn, cinnamon, cloves, and bay leaf, reduce the heat. Gently stir.
15. Add chicken, cook, stirring for 5-8 mins, until the chicken turns opaque.

Make the onion paste:

16. In a blender or food processor, add the fried onions and a couple of tablespoons of water.
17. Pulse until it becomes a coarse paste.
18. Add the fried onion paste, salt, and coriander to the pot with the chicken.
19. Mix everything together.
20. Cover and let it simmer for 5-8 minutes or until the chicken is cooked through.

Assemble the dish:

21. Remove the lid.
22. Add the yogurt, almond paste, and shredded coconut (if using).
23. Stir well.
24. Cook, uncovered, on medium-high heat for another 2-3 minutes, until the sauce turns creamy and the oil starts to separate.
25. Garnish with almonds and fresh coriander.
26. Serve with hot naan .

Cucumber Raita

A cooling accompaniment to Indian food

Prep Time	Cook Time	Total Time	Servings
5 mins	5 mins	10 mins	6

Ingredients

¾ cup whole milk plain yogurt
½ cup finely diced or grated cucumber seeds removed
tblspn finely chopped greentops of spring onion
2 teaspoons lemon or lime juice,
1 tablespoon olive oil
½ teaspoon ground cumin seeds,
½ teaspoon ground coriander seeds,
2–3 tablespoons chopped mint
2–3 tablespoons chopped coriander
¼ teaspoon salt, more to taste
¼ teaspoon pepper

Method

1. Place all ingredients in a bowl and stir.
2. Refrigerate until ready to serve.
3. Garnish with fresh herbs.

Tandoori Chicken

If you have a Tandoor, great! But a barbecue grill works well too!

Prep Time	Cook Time	Total Time	Servings
15 mins	50 mins + chilling	65 min + chilling	4

A tandoor is a traditional wood-fired oven used across Asia. Modern versions of the tandoor are available as charcoal fired, stainless steel appliances.

This recipe is designed for a BBQ/grill. It's ideal for a Weber Kettle BBQ

Ingredients

3 tablespoons vegetable oil
1 teaspoon ground coriander
1 teaspoon ground cumin
1 teaspoon ground turmeric
1 teaspoon cayenne
1 tablespoon garam masala
1 tablespoon sweet (not hot) paprika
1 cup plain yogurt (can sub buttermilk)
2 tablespoons lemon juice
2 tablespoons minced fresh ginger
1 teaspoon salt
4 whole chicken leg quarters (drumsticks and thighs), skinless, bone-in.

Method

1. Heat the oil in a small pan at medium heat
2. Cook the coriander, cumin, turmeric, cayenne, garam masala and paprika, stirring often, until fragrant, 2-3 mins
3. Allow to completely cool.
4. Whisk the cooled spice-oil mixture into the yogurt, mix in the lemon juice, salt and ginger.
5. Cut 2-3 deep slashes to the bone ion the leg/thigh pieces.
6. Coat the chicken in the marinade, cover and chill for 6-8 hrs, no longer.
7. Prepare your grill ; one side over direct heat, the other not over direct heat.
8. Lightly spray grill with vegetable oil.
9. Take the chicken out of the marinade and shake off the excess.
10. The chicken should be coated, but not dripping with marinade.
11. Put the chicken pieces on the hot side of the grill and cover. Cook 2-3 mins.
12. Turn the chicken so it is brown on all sides. A little charring is great!
13. Move chicken to the cool side of the grill. Cover and cook for 20-40 minutes, or longer depending on the size of the chicken and the temperature of the grill.
14. The chicken is done when its juices run clear.
15. Rest for at least 5 minutes before serving.

*Serve with naan,
or with Indian style rice,
with yogurt-based raita on the side.*

Essentials for Asian Cooking

Find a good Asian grocery shop in your area. You will find all the staples there and lots of great advice. Ask for garlic free and if the labels are in an Asian language, ask the grocer to translate for you, if he/she can.

If you are shopping in Woolworths or Coles, go to the online store before you go shopping in store. The online shopping site gives you the ingredients of each item. You can check which brands are garlic free.

Equipment

Wok

The wok is the most important piece of equipment. It is most commonly used for stir frying, but can also be used to steam, braise, fry, simmer and smoke food. Most woks are made of cast iron or carbon steel. The wok has a round bottom that receives a higher concentration of heat than the sides, allowing the cook to toss the hot food from the middle into the cooler sides of the pan, which is the ideal cooking method for stir fries.

Wok Spatula

A wok spatula is designed with a curved blade so that it can reach food in the rounded bottom and sides of the wok. It is the ideal utensil for stir frying. It has a long handle so that cooks will not burn their hands.

Wok Ladle

Like the wok spatula, the curved bottom of a wok ladle has the perfect shape to reach into the bottom of the wok. Solid ladles are used to stir-fry and serve soups, broths or sauce-rich foods out of the wok. Perforated ladles can be used for collecting vegetables, meats and noodles that have been cooking in broth or sauce in the pan.

Wok Brush

A wok brush is a wooden brush with stiff, thick bristles that are used to scrape and clean the inside of a wok. The brush is made with long bristles so that it is flexible enough to clean the rounded surface.

Bamboo Steamer

Many foods require you to use a steamer. Both traditional bamboo and contemporary steel steamers are available.

Hot Pot

Used for cooking and serving food at the tabletop, a hotpot has a narrow bottom and a wide top rim. Usually, the pot is filled with broth, coconut milk or another liquid. Ingredients are then placed in the pot and are cooked at the table. Hot pots without a space for fuel and a flame are also available for cooking on a stovetop or in an oven

Ginger Grater

A ginger grater is a must-have item. Grating ginger before it is added to stir fries, soups and other dishes helps to release the flavours and juices of the ginger.

Spices

If you keep the same spices as for Indian cooking, you can't go wrong. Just add Szechuan Peppercorns to the list.

Light and dark soy sauce (or Tamari for gluten free): Light soy sauce is amber in colour, thinner and saltier. The more common dark soy sauce has more body. It is thicker and less salty.

Rice vinegar A mild vinegar great for vinaigrettes, quick pickles, dipping sauces.

Shoaxing Chinese Wine/ Japanese Rice Wine

Miso Great in soups, dressings, marinades and light sauces. It can even be used in place of dairy in some recipes.

Hoisin Sauce A sweet and savoury past; a glaze for meat, an addition to stir fries, or as dipping sauce. Hoisin usually includes soy, red chillies and garlic. See our recipe for GaF Hoisin sauce

Red and Green Curry Paste See our garlic free recipes.

Mirin A sweet rice wine used in marinades and sauces.

Linghams Chili Sauce A substitute for Sriracha & Chinese Chili Sauce (Available Woolworths)

Fish sauce A salty sauce essential in East and Southeast Asian cuisine

Shrimp paste (Blaken) Smells terrible, but adds lots of flavour.

Oyster sauce: Great in stir fries and fried rice.

Sesame seeds (white and black)

Rice Basmati and Thai jasmine rice are the ones most often used.

Noodles Soba and udon for soups. Egg and Rice noodles for accompaniments and in stir fries.

Wonton Wrappers (Square and round) and

Spring Roll Wrappers (Rice and egg noodle)

Fresh ingredients

Bean sprouts

Bok Choy / Pak Choy

Broccoli

Carrots

Chili - There are many varieties that vary greatly in heat. Choose one suited to the recipe and your taste.

Chinese Cabbage

Coriander

Galangal

Ginger

Lemongrass

Limes

Korean dumplings

No matter how you cook them, these are little bites of heaven!

Prep Time	Cook Time	Total Time	Servings
30 mins	30 mins	1 hr	22 dumplings

Ingredients

Filling
500g lean beef/pork mince
1 medium spring onion/leek, finely chopped
1 cup finely chopped parboiled cabbage
½ cup chopped tofu (1 small cake)
4 ounces mung bean noodles
2 tablespoons soy sauce
1 tablespoon sesame oil
1 teaspoon salt
1 teaspoon ground black pepper
1 packet round Chinese wonton wrappers

Dumpling dipping sauce
⅓ cup soy sauce
⅓ cup rice wine vinegar
1 tablespoon sesame oil
1 tablespoon chili flakes
1 tablespoon thinly sliced scallions

Recipe Note
Korean dumplings are traditionally made with a beef or pork filling, but you can substitute chicken, prawn or vegetables.

Method

1. Soak mung bean noodles in hot water for 15 mins and then chop.
2. In a mixing bowl, combine the beef / pork, spring onion, cabbage, tofu, and noodles.
3. In a separate small bowl, combine the soy sauce, sesame oil, salt, and pepper.
4. Pour seasoning mixture over meat and vegetables and mix with hands.
5. Place about 1 tblspn of filling in the centre of a dumpling wrapper.
6. Fold the wrapper in half, pressing to seal and then crimp the edges.
7. Repeat until the filling is gone.
8. You can steam, boil, steam, pan fry, or deep fry the dumplings as you wish.

To boil bring pot half full of water to a boil and gently slide them in. When it returns to a boil, turn the heat down - simmer 6 -8 mins.

To steam place in a steamer basket. Steam for 15-20 mins.

To pan-fry place 2 tablespoons of vegetable oil in a pan at medium-high heat. Cook 2-3 mins per side, or until golden brown.

To deep-fry heat a few inches of canola oil in a deep fryer or frypan. Fry in batches for 2-3 minutes, until golden brown.

Sauce
9. Place all the dipping sauce ingredients together in a bowl.
10. Mix well.

Serve the dumplings with the dipping sauce.

Steamed Barramundi and Mushroom Rice

Delicious!! A lovely blend of Australian and Asian flavours.

Prep Time	Cook Time	Total Time	Servings
10 mins	20 mins	30 mins	4

Ingredients

4 skinless barramundi fillets (200gm each)
70 ml Chinese Cooking wine
2 tbsp soy sauce
2 tsp sesame oil
30 gm ginger, cut into julienne
1 tbsp vegetable oil
100 gm Swiss Brown mushrooms, thickly sliced
Green tops of 3 spring onions, thinly sliced
1 tbsp finely grated ginger
1 cup jasmine rice
2 cups hot GaF chicken stock
1 tbsp soy sauce

Serve on a bed of mushroom rice scattered with spring onion and crushed macadamia nuts.

Method

For mushroom rice

1. Heat oil in a saucepan over medium heat
2. Add mushrooms, spring onion and ginger and sauté until just tender (2-3 minutes)
3. Add rice and stir to coat.
4. Add stock, soy sauce and 2 tbsp water, bring to the boil, cover with a tight-fitting lid
5. Reduce heat to low and cook for 10 mins.
6. Remove from heat and stand for 5 mins.

Meanwhile;

7. Place fish on a plate in a steamer basket,
8. Drizzle with Chinese Cooking wine, soy sauce and sesame oil, top with ginger and season to taste.
9. Cover and steam over a saucepan of boiling water until fish is opaque (4-5 minutes).

Vietnamese Prawn Spring Rolls

No deep frying and to die for!!

Prep Time	Cook Time	Total Time	Servings
10 mins - + Peel Prawns	20 mins - assembly	30 - 40 mins	**22 rolls**

Ingredients

100g rice vermicelli noodles
250g pkt 22cm rice paper sheets
22 cooked medium prawns peeled and halved lengthways
1 red capsicum, seeded, cut into thin strips
3 spring onions, cut into 8cm lengths
⅓ cup (80ml) sweet chilli sauce
2 tbsp lime juice
Mint leaves, extra, to serve

Sweet Chili Sauce

Sweet Chili Sauce that you buy contains garlic. This is GaF Sweet Chili Sauce that is just as nice, if not nicer.

⅓ cup rice vinegar
⅓ cup water
⅓ cup + 2 tablespoons cane sugar
1 tblspns rice wine (or dry sherry)
1 tablespoon Sambal Oelek. Use more or less according to taste start with less and add more if desired.
1 teaspoon finely minced ginger
1 teaspoon tamari or soy sauce (use tamari for gluten free)
2 teaspoons cornflour dissolved in 1 tablespoon water to make a thin paste

Serve the rice paper rolls with the sweet chili dipping sauce and extra mint

Method

1. Place the noodles in a large heatproof bowl. Cover with boiling water. Stand for 5 mins or until noodles soften.
2. Refresh under cold water. Drain.
3. Fill a shallow dish with warm water.
4. Dip a rice paper sheet in water.
5. Drain and place on a clean board - it will continue to soften.
6. Arrange 2 prawn halves, 1 mint leaf, 1 piece capsicum, 1 piece spring onion and some of the noodles in the centre of the rice paper sheet.
7. Fold the bottom half of wrapper over filling. Fold the sides over, then roll to enclose.
8. Place on a large tray.
9. Repeat with remaining rice paper sheets, and filling
10. Place the rolls slightly apart on the tray to stop them sticking to each other.

Sweet Chili Sauce

11. Place all of the ingredients except for the cornflour paste in a small saucepan and bring it to a boil, stirring regularly.
12. Once the sugar is dissolved stir in the cornflour, stirring until thickened.
13. Let the sauce cool completely, pour into an airtight jar and store in the refrigerator.
14. Will keep for up to a week.
15. Makes about 1 cup
16. Combine the sweet chilli sauce and lime juice in a small bowl.

Thai Coconut Soup

Use the garlic free red curry paste for a lovely soup.

Prep Time	Cook Time	Total Time	Servings
15 mins	30 mins + curry paste	45 mins	4

½ tablespoon vegetable oil
1 tablespoon grated fresh ginger
½ stalk lemon grass, minced
1 teaspoons red curry paste (below).
2 cups chicken stock
1 ½ tablespoons fish sauce
½ tablespoon light brown sugar
1 ½ cans coconut milk
125gm shiitake mushrooms, sliced
500 gm medium prawns – peeled and deveined
1 tblspn fresh lime juice
salt to taste

1. Heat the oil in a large pot over medium heat.
2. Cook and stir the ginger, lemongrass, and curry paste or 1 minute.
3. Slowly pour the chicken broth over the mixture, stirring continuously.
4. Stir in the fish sauce and brown sugar; simmer for 15 minutes.
5. Stir in the coconut milk and mushrooms; cook and stir until the mushrooms are soft, about 5 minutes.
6. Add the shrimp; cook about 5 mins.
7. Stir in the lime juice; season with salt;
8. Garnish with fresh coriander

Garlic Free Red Curry Paste

Thai flavour without garlic

Prep Time	Cook Time	Total Time	Servings
10 mins	N/A	10 mins	N/A

Ingredients

Red chili peppers to taste (1 very mild, 5 HOT)
2 cups green tops of spring onions cut into chunks
2 tblspns chopped coriander
1 tblspn vegetable oil
1 tblspn ground coriander
2 tspns lemon zest
2 tspns ground cumin
2 tspns shrimp paste
2 tspns paprika
1 tspn whole black peppercorns
1 tspn lemongrass powder
1 tspn turmeric
1 tspn salt.

Method

1. Blend chili peppers, spring onions, coriander, oil, coriander, lemon zest, cumin, shrimp paste, paprika, peppercorns, lemon grass, turmeric, and salt together in a blender until a smooth, paste-like consistency is reached.

For garlic intolerance:

If you enjoy garlic flavour, you can safely substitute garlic infused oil for ¼ of the vegetable oil.

Beef in Oyster Sauce

The lovely thing about oyster sauce is it's traditionally garlic free.

Prep Time	Cook Time	Total Time	Servings
10 mins + marinating	10 mins	20 mins	4

Ingredients

450g lean beef steak cut into 5cm x 5mm strips
1 tbsp light soy sauce
2 tsp sesame oil
1 tbsp Chinese cooking wine
2 tsp cornflour
3 tbsp peanut oil
1 red capsicum cut into chunky dice
1 green capsicum, cut into chunky dice
3 tbsp oyster sauce
2 spring onions, finely shredded, to garnish

Method

Cook the beef
1. Cut the beef strips *against the grain of the meat*.
2. Put them in a bowl.
3. Mix in the soy sauce, sesame oil, wine and cornflour.
4. Leave to marinate for at least 20 mins.
5. Heat a wok until it is very hot
6. Add the peanut oil.
7. When the oil is slightly smoking, add the beef slices and stir-fry for 5 mins or until lightly browned.
8. Remove the meat from the wok and drain well in a colander set inside a bowl.
9. Discard the drained oil.

Cook the vegetable
10. Wipe the wok clean and reheat it over a high heat.
11. Add the capsicum, and cook for 3-4 mins or until softened.
12. Add the oyster sauce and bring to a simmer.

Assemble the dish
13. Return the drained beef slices to the wok and toss them thoroughly with the oyster sauce.
14. Turn the mixture on to a serving platter,
15. Top with the spring onions and serve immediately.

Prawn Chow Mein, Soft Noodles

My absolute favourite!

Prep Time	Cook Time	Total Time	Servings
15 mins	15 mins	30 mins	4

If you like your Chow Mein with crispy noodles, they are available pre-cooked at any supermarket in the Asian Foods section. Simply great warm them in the microwave according to the packet instructions and serve them on the side after plating the dish.

Ingredients

500g medium egg noodles
1 tbsp sesame oil
2 tbsp peanut/vegetable oil
1 inch piece of fresh ginger finely grated
16 fresh raw king prawns, peeled and de-veined
200g snow peas, thoroughly washed
1 carrot thinly sliced crossways
A handful of small broccoli florets
2 tbsp Chinese cooking wine or dry sherry
2 tbsp light soy sauce
2 tbsp dark soy sauce
Salt and ground white pepper
2 spring onions, finely shredded into 4cm long strips

Method

1. Cook the noodles according to the packet instructions,.
2. Drain and tip into a bowl. Pour over the sesame oil, tossing thoroughly to coat the noodles. Put to one side.
3. Heat the peanut/vegetable oil in a wok over a high heat.
4. Once hot, stir-fry the grated ginger for a few seconds before adding the prawns - **do not allow the ginger to burn.**
5. Add the prawns, continuing to stir-fry for 2-3 minutes. The prawns should be pink and a little brown on some of the edges.
6. Remove the prawns and set to one side.
7. Add the snow peas, carrots and broccoli and stir-fry 3-4 mins.
8. Return the prawns to the wok and mix to incorporate.
9. Pour in the wine and leave to almost evaporate before adding the cooked and reserved noodles.
10. Toss so that all of the ingredients are well mixed.
11. Turn the heat down to medium .
12. Add both of the soy sauces and a pinch of salt and pepper.
13. Stir-fry for a further 2 minutes before spooning on to a plate and dressing with the spring onions .

Malay Prawn Soup

There is optional garlic infused oil in this recipe.

Prep Time	Cook Time	Total Time	Servings

Ingredients

2 tbsp peanut oil in
Optional 1 tspn garlic infused olive oil.
12 large uncooked banana prawns
Heads & shells of uncooked prawns.
12 cups GaF fish stock or GaF Prawn Stock*
2 tspns Sambal Oelek
2 tsp palm sugar
Pinch of salt
150g pork
300g pork bones
150g rice vermicelli noodles
3 eggs, hard boiled, shelled and cut in quarters lengthwise
6 large Lettuce leaves blanched

Follow the Step 2 of the cooking instructions to the letter.

Do not break the garlic and remove it from the oil prior to Step 3.

Recipe Note

This recipe is even more delicious if, whenever you have prawns, cooked or raw, you save the heads and shells and freeze them Defrost a couple of handfuls and add them to the shells from your fresh green prawns.

Method

1. Peel and devein prawns - save heads and shells
2. Put oil and garlic infused oil in pan.
3. Gently stir fry the prawns in the oil until they turn pink and are slightly charred.
4. Remove the prawns and set aside.
5. Add the prawn heads and shells. Stir fry until starting to brown.
6. Add 8 cups fish stock, palm sugar, sambal and salt .
7. Bring to the boil and simmer for up to 2 hours or until the stock is reduced to 8 cups of liquid.
8. Strain the stock and remove the prawn heads and shells.
9. Place the pan back on the heat and add the pork meat and bones.
10. Cook until the meat is just cooked.
11. Remove the meat and bones.
12. Cut the meat into slices and return to the soup.
13. Cook for a further 20 minutes.
14. In a separate saucepan scald the noodles in boiling water.
15. Drain, and place ⅓ of the noodles each into 4 deep soup bowls.
16. Place the egg, prawns, pork and lettuce on top of the noodles.
17. Pour the soup mixture over the top.
18. To serve, add extra sambal to taste and briefly stir.

See GaF Fish Stock and GaF Prawn Stock recipes p. 16

Garlic Free Hoisin Sauce
Essential for glazes and BBQ sauces

Prep Time	Cook Time	Total Time	Servings
10 mins	-	10 mins	N/A

Ingredients

4 tablespoons soy sauce
2 tablespoons black bean paste (available from Asian grocery in a can)
1 tablespoon molasses or 1 tablespoon honey
1 tspn Linghams Chili Sauce (available from Woolies)
2 teaspoons seasoned rice vinegar
2 teaspoons sesame oil
⅛ teaspoon Szechuan peppercorns ground

Method

1. Combine all ingredients in a small mixing bowl.
2. Mix with a whisk until well blended

Recipe Note

Don't be put off by the size of the Black Bean Paste can, you can transfer leftover paste to a suitable container and freeze for use another time.

If you can't find Black Bean Paste, substitute peanut butter, but it isn't nearly as nice and has a much lighter colour.

Garlic Free Gochujang Paste
Essential in Korean dishes.

Prep Time	Cook Time	Total Time	Servings
10 mins	-	10 mins	N/A

Ingredients

½ cup white miso paste
¼ cup honey
Tblspn cayenne pepper, or less to taste
2 tablespoons mirin
1 tablespoon caster sugar

Method

1. Stir together the miso, honey, cayenne pepper, mirin, and sugar until well combined.
2. Decant the gochujang mixture into a clean jar or resealable container,.
3. Cover, and place in the refrigerator
4. Will keep for up to three weeks.
5. You can use the gochujang immediately but the flavour is best if you leave it a day or two.

Korean Bibimbap

Beef with vegetables and rice Korean style - delicious

Prep Time	Cook Time	Total Time	Servings
20 mins	15 - 20 mins	40 mins	3-4

Ingredients

100g beef mince
1 tbsp soy sauce
1tbsp sesame oil
1 tsp dark brown sugar
250g mildly seasoned spinach
350g mildly seasoned bean sprouts
100g shiitake mushroom thinly sliced
1 small carrot peeled and julienned
2 x ¼ tsp fine sea salt 3 to 4 serving portions of steamed rice (pre-cooked and hot))
3 or 4 eggs (1 person)
Cooking oil to cook the meat, mushroom, carrots and eggs
Korean seasoned seaweed*, shredded (long thin cut)

Bibimbap Sauce

2 tbsp gochujang (see facing page)
1 tbsp sesame oil
1 tbsp sugar
1 tbsp water
1 tbsp roasted sesame seeds
1 tsp apple vinegar

As each component is cooked, keep hot until the dish is ready to assemble.

Recipe Note

A traditional accompaniment to this dish is Kimchi. While most people find this delicious fermented cabbage fantastic to eat, –it's the bringer of misery to the garlic intolerant. The fermentation process includes garlic.

Method

Meat

1. Mix the beef mince with the meat sauce (soy and sesame oil)
2. Marinate the meat for about 30 mins
3. Add some cooking oil into a wok and cook the meat on medium high to high heat for 3-5 mins until cooked.

Vegetables

4. Add some cooking oil and ¼ tsp of fine sea salt in a wok
5. Cook the carrots on medium high to high heat for 2 to 3 mins. Put aside and keep warm.
6. Wipe out the wok and add some cooking oil and 1/4 tsp of fine sea salt to it.
7. Cook the mushrooms on medium high to high heat 2-3 mins until they are all cooked. Put aside and keep warm.
8. Fry eggs to your preference.

Bibimbap Sauce

9. Mix the Bibimbap sauce ingredients in a bowl. Set aside

Assemble

10. Put the rice into a bowl and add the meat, assorted cooked and raw vegetables, seasoned seaweed, Bibimbap sauce and the egg on top of the rice.
11. Mix the ingredients well in the bowl and enjoy!

*The Korean Seaweed is available at specialist Korean or Asian grocery shops.

Prawn Wontons

Wonton Soup made with GaF Chicken Stock (page 14)

Prep Time	Cook Time	Total Time	Servings
30 mins	30 mins	1 hr	

Ingredients

1 tblspn light soy sauce
1 tblspn julienne ginger
1 tspn white sugar
1 tspn sesame oil
2 bok choy,
Thinly sliced spring onion, to serve

For the stock
1.5 litres of GaF Chicken Stock (p14)
8 spring onions
Large pice of fresh ginger root

For the Wontons
300 gm uncooked king prawns, peeled, cut into approx 2 cm slices
1 tbsp thinly sliced spring onion
1 tsp finely diced ginger
1 tsp Chinese cooking wine
1 tsp light soy sauce
1 tsp white sugar
1 tsp sesame oil
16 square wonton wrappers

Method

Stock
1. Cut the spring onions in half.
2. Cut 6 x 2mm slices off the ginger root.
3. In a large saucepan combine the GaF stock, spring onions and ginger.
4. Bring to a simmer and cook for 15 mins.
5. Strain the stock through muslin or a new Chux cloth.

Wontons
6. Combine all the wonton ingredients (except wrappers) in a bowl
7. Cover and marinate in the fridge for 30 minutes .
8. Place heaped tspn of prawn mixture in the centre of each wrapper.
9. Dampen the edges with a little water.
10. Fold over to form a triangle.
11. Press edges to push out any air and seal.
12. Dampen one corner with water, then bring corners to the middle and press them together.
13. Place on a tray lined with baking paper and cover .

Assemble the dish
14. Bring 1.5 litres stock to the boil in a large saucepan.
15. Add soy, ginger, sugar and sesame oil and reduce to a simmer.
16. Add wontons and simmer for 2 minutes,
17. Add bok choy and simmer until wontons are cooked through (1-2 minutes).
18. Divide soup, wontons and bok choy among bowls, scatter with spring onion and serve hot.

Green Rice Crusted Prawns & Plum Sauce

A very nice, very unusual Vietnamese entrée

Prep Time	Cook Time	Total Time	Servings
30 mins	20 mins	50 mins	4

This recipe can be adapted to make coconut prawns. Simply substitute shredded coconut for the rice flakes.

Ingredients

Prawns
175g green rice flakes (from Vietnamese food shops) – or substitute rice flakes from health food shop.
16 large green prawns, peeled, tail on and deveined
Sunflower oil, to deep fry

Plum Sauce
300g plums, stones removed, and chopped (or tin of plums drained)
70g caster sugar
8cm piece ginger peeled, sliced
2/3 cup rice wine vinegar
1/3 cup light soy sauce

To serve
Ground lemon myrtle
Lime wedges
Plum sauce

Serve the prawns with lime wedges and the plum sauce.

Method

Prawns

1. To prepare the prawns, place rice flakes in a shallow dish.
2. Peel each prawn and immediately roll it in rice flakes, pressing them to stick to the prawn.
3. Half-fill a deep-fryer or large saucepan
4. with oil and heat to 180°C.
5. In 2 batches, deep-fry the prawns, turning halfway, for 2 minutes or until golden and cooked through.
6. Remove with a slotted spoon and drain on paper towel.
7. While hot, transfer to a serving platter and season with a pinch of salt flakes and lemon myrtle.
8. Place the plums in a blender and whiz until smooth.
9. Place sugar in a frypan over medium-high heat.
10. Cook, swirling the pan occasionally to dissolve the sugar, until it turns to a golden caramel.
11. Add ginger, vinegar and soy (the sugar will harden, but it will re-dissolve over heat).
12. Add plum purée and bring to a simmer, stirring occasionally, until reduced by one-third.
13. Strain through a sieve into a heatproof bowl and cool.

Middle Eastern

Essential Middle Eastern Ingredients

Middle Eastern cuisine includes Arab, Armenian, Assyrian, Azerbaijani, Cypriot, Georgian, Iranian, Israeli, Kurdish, Moroccan and Turkish cuisines. Hospitality is central to Middle Eastern culture and many home cooks spend hours, sometimes days, preparing an impressive spread of dishes for family feasts.

Middle Eastern food is all about fresh ingredients, lots of vegetables and grains. Fried foods are rare, instead cooking involves baking, grilling, and using raw ingredients. This type of cuisine is considered healthier than the usual modern diet.

Grains are the basis of the Middle Eastern diet, where wheat and rice are staple foods. Barley is widely used in the region. Bread is a universal food eaten in some form by all classes at nearly every meal., Burghul, cracked wheat, is cooked in water with flavorings, much like rice, or used in meat pies and as an ingredient in salads. Freekeh is another common grain, made from immature green wheat. Butter and clarified butter are traditionally the preferred medium of cooking.

Most regions in the Middle East use spices. A typical stew will include a small amount of cinnamon, nutmeg, cloves, cumin, and coriander. Black pepper is popular and chili is used occasionally, especially as a sauce or as pickles. Parsley and mint are widely used in cooking and in salads.

Thyme and thyme blends (za'atar) are common in Syria, Lebanon, Jordan, Palestine and Israel, besides a mixture of dried thyme and sumac (crushed sour berries). Sumac is also sprinkled over grilled meat, and they frequently used garlic in many dishes and salads.

Lamb and mutton are most consumed meats, since both Islamic and Jewish dietary laws prohibit pork. Grilled meats are popular, with many regional varieties. Meat and vegetable stews are served with rice, bulgur, or bread.

Vegetables and pulses are staple foods. Leaf vegetables include many varieties of cabbage, spinach, and chard. Root vegetables, such as onions, garlic, carrots, turnips, and beets are vegetable staples. As are squash, tomato, eggplant, and okra. Tomato is a popular ingredient in Middle-Eastern cookery, used fresh in salads, cooked in stews and broth, and grilled.

Beans and pulses are crucial to the Middle Eastern diet. Broad beans are eaten both green and dried. Lentils, split peas and chickpeas are widely used in soups and salads, with rice or meat.

butter	olive oil	rice	cheese
clarified butter	pita	chickpeas	yoghurt
burghul	freekeh	lentils	Split peas
rose water	honey	dried fruits	filo pastry

Cooking & Eating in a Garlic-Free Zone

Basic pantry and fridge ingredients

Essential Spices and herbs

Baharat[1]	mint	saffron
black pepper,	nutmeg	sumac[2]
cinnamon	paprika	thyme
coriander	parsley	Za'atar[3]
cumin	Ras el Hanout	
ginger	dried rose buds	

Beware - *Many Woolworths and Coles own brand herbs and spices, and Masterfoods Morrocan, Harrisa and other Middle Eastern blend spices contain garlic crystals, flakes or powder.* **Read all labels.**

Vegetables and fruit

beans	capsicum red and green	figs
okra	eggplant	dates
cabbage	broad beans	pomegranates
vine leaves	beetroot	apricots
olives	Spinach	pistachio
cucumbers	lemons	almonds

[1]**Baharat** is a spice mix of black pepper, coriander, paprika, cardamom, nutmeg, cumin, cloves, and cinnamon. Other spices that can be a part of baharat are sumac, saffron, chili and turmeric. The recipe to make your own is on the following page.

[2]**Sumac** is made from the dried and ground berries of the wild sumac flower. It is a tangy spice with a sour, acidic flavor somewhat like lemon juice. Fantastic on fish.

[3]**Za'atar** is a blend of dried thyme, oregano, marjoram, sumac, toasted sesame seeds, and salt,

All three of these spices can be found, ready mixed, at supermarkets or specialist food retailers who stock **Malouf's Spice Mezza** *brand. Malouf's have GaF Baharat, Sumac and Ras el Hanout.*

The jars are very recogniseable.

Baharat
Make it yourself spice mixture

Prep Time	Cook Time	Total Time	Servings
5 mins	N/A	5 mins	N/A

Ingredients

2 tsp paprika
2 tsp ground cumin
1 tsp freshly ground black pepper
1 tsp ground coriander
1/2 tsp ground cinnamon
1/2 tsp ground nutmeg
1/4 tsp ground cardamom
1/4 tsp ground cloves

Method

1. Heat a small skillet over medium-high heat and dry roast the cumin, pepper, coriander, cardamom and cloves until they become very fragrant, about 3-5 minutes, tossing regularly to prevent scorching.
2. Transfer them to a bowl and allow them to cool completely before grinding them in a spice or coffee grinder along with the paprika, cinnamon and nutmeg.
3. Keep stored in an airtight glass jar.

Za'atar
Make it yourself spice mixture

Prep Time	Cook Time	Total Time	Servings
10 mins	N/A	10 mins	N/A

Ingredients

1 tablespoon roasted sesame seeds
1/4 cup ground sumac
2 tablespoons dried thyme
2 tablespoons dried marjoram
2 tablespoons dried oregano
1 teaspoon coarse salt

Method

1. Grind the roasted sesame seeds in a spice/coffee grinder.
2. Mix all the spices together in a small bowl.
3. Place the left over Za'atar in a spice jar with a good seal. Will keep for at least a month.

Baked Fish Lebanese Style

A delicious fusion of Australian fish and Eastern flavours

Prep Time	Cook Time	Total Time	Servings
20 mins	30 mins	50 mins	4

Ingredients

1 whole firm fish, about 1.5kg, cleaned and descaled (snapper, coral trout, blue eyed trevally, barramundi)
2 tspns Sumac
1 green capsicum, thinly sliced
1 red capsicum, thinly sliced
Juice of 2 lemons
1 sliced lemon
1 tblspn chopped fresh thyme
1 tblspn chopped fresh coriander
3 tblspns za'atar
5 tspns olive oil (or 1 tspn garlic infused oil and 4 tspns olive oil)
1 tspn salt or to taste

Method

1. Rinse the fish, ensure cavity is clean.
2. Rub with a little salt and 2 tspns Sumac.
3. Place several slices of lemon in the cavity.
4. Bake 20 minutes at 180C.

While the fish is baking:-

5. Mix lemon juice, thyme, coriander, za'atar, oil and salt., Creating a thick red paste.
6. Mix with the sliced capsicum.

Assemble the dish

7. Once the fish is baked, remove the bones and skin. (Leave the oven on.)
8. Break up the meat into large chunks and place it in a heat proof baking dish.
9. Cover the top of the fish with the paste.
10. Return to the oven for about 10 minutes to allow the fish to absorb the paste.
11. Serve hot or cold with couscous, rice, or salad.

Beef Fatteh

A 'must eat with your fingers' traditional dish

Prep Time	Cook Time	Total Time	Servings
15 mins	1 hr	75 mins	6

Ingredients

4 pitta breads split and cut into nacho-sized triangles

For the topping
500 grams full-fat greek yoghurt
5 x 15ml tablespoons tahini (at room temperature)
1 - 2 lemons (to give 3 x 15ml tablespoons of juice)
1 - 2 teaspoons sea salt flakes (to taste)

For the Eggplant Layer
3 x 15ml tblspns olive oil
Green tops of 1 spring onion, finely chopped
1 medium-large eggplant cut into small cubes
2 teaspoons ground cumin
2 teaspoons ground coriander
1 teaspoon barabat
1 - 2 tspns sea salt flakes
500 grams minced beef

To sprinkle on top
125 grams pomegranate seeds
50 grams toasted pine nuts
1 tablespoon finely shredded mint leaves

Method

1. Preheat the oven to 200°C/180°C Fan
2. Spread the pitta triangles on a large baking sheet and toast 10–15 mins .
3. Set the pitta triangles aside.
4. Beat the yogurt, tahini, lemon juice, and 1 tspn of sea salt flakes together in a heatproof bowl. Put to one side.
5. Warm the oil in a wide, heavy-based pan and cook the spring onion over a med-low heat, stirring for 5 mins. Turn the heat down and cook until soft.
6. Turn the heat up to medium, add the eggplant stirring well. Cook for about 10 minutes, stirring constantly.
7. Stir in the cumin, coriander and tspn each of pepper and sea salt.
8. Over a high heat, add the mince, break it up a little and turn in the pan until seared.
9. Turn heat back to medium and cook 10 mins, stirring occasionally, until the meat is cooked. Taste for seasoning.
10. Take off the heat. Put to one side.
11. Pour some just-boiled water into a fresh pan and place over a low heat.
12. Sit the bowl with the tahini-yogurt mixture on top, making sure the bowl does not touch the water.
13. Beat well until the yogurt is slightly above room temperature.

Assemble

Arrange the pitta triangles on a large platter. Top with the eggplant-beef mixture, then the yogurt-tahini sauce. Sprinkle with barabat. Scatter the pomegranate seeds, toasted pine nuts and, finely shredded mint.

Baba Ganoush

Careful! This smokey, gorgeous dip is addictive.

Prep Time	Cook Time	Total Time	Servings
15 mins	10 mins	25 mins	N/A

Ingredients

4 Lebanese eggplants (or 2 large egg-shaped eggplants) approx 1 kg
1 lemon
Tspn garlic infused oil (optional)
1 tsp salt
½ cup of tahini
1 tblspn extra virgin olive oil

Method

1. Char the eggplants. Turn every few minutes until well done.
2. Put the eggplants in a colander to drain and remove the burnt skin with a fork. Cut the tops off.
3. Put the eggplant in a bowl and beat well with a pestle or the bottom of a sturdy cup. (Using a pestle keeps a grainy texture).
4. Add the lemon, tahini, salt and garlic infused oil and mix. Adjust seasoning if necessary.
5. Drizzle with the extra virgin olive oil just before serving.

Lebanese Eggplant

Egg-shaped Eggplant

Recipe Note

I prefer the longer, more slender, Lebanese eggplant. We grow them in our veggie patch. They are prolific bearers. The crop is always too much to use immediately, but I find they are easy to bake and freeze for later use.

I have given you the weight so that you can choose the more familiar egg plant if you wish.

To get the smoky flavour that is authentic Lebanese Baba Ganoush, it is best to char the eggplant on a gas hob. It's a messy process but worth it.

If, however, you don't have a gas hob, bake the eggplants in the oven until they start to char.

Prawn Börek

A different take on a Turkish favourite

Prep Time	Cook Time	Total Time	Servings
20 mins	10 mins	30 mins	4

Recipe Note

Borek is thinly rolled pastry, usually filo, wrapped around various savoury fillings or arranged in layers. There are a myriad types of borek; triangles, rolled sausage shaped, cigar shaped and layered slices, filled with cheeses, minced meats or prawns, and vegetables. They can be fried, baked, cooked on a griddle or boiled.

Traditionally it was said that no girl should marry until she had mastered the art of börek making. Böreks should be light and crisp, without a trace of excess oil. It's one of the most traditional pastry dishes in Turkey that can be eaten any time of the day from breakfast to dinner, either as a main dish, appetizer, or snack.

Ingredients

8 large uncooked king prawns, peeled, deveined and finely chopped
200 gm halloumi, coarsely grated
200 gm Greek sheep's feta, coarsely grated
4 tbsp finely chopped flat-leaf parsley
½ tsp cayenne pepper
4 egg yolks
8 filo pastry sheets
Vegetable oil, for deep-frying
2 tsp nigella seeds

Method

1. Combine prawns with cheeses, parsley and cayenne pepper, then fold through yolks.
2. Place the filo sheets, baking sheet, a bowl with olive oil and a pastry brush on the table.
3. Spread a filo strip on the table.
4. Brush it gently with olive oil.
5. Fold over lengthways.
6. Place 2 tblspn of filling at one end
7. Fold one corner of pastry over the filling to form a triangle.
8. Repeat folding from side to side in a triangle shape until there is one fold left.
9. Brush end with water, make the last fold and press to seal and form a triangular parcel.
10. Repeat with remaining fillo sheets and filling and refrigerate for 1 hour uncovered.
11. Heat oil in a large deep saucepan to 180°C.
12. Deep-fry börek, in batches, turning occasionally, until golden and cooked through (3-4 mins).
13. Drain on paper towels, sprinkle with nigella seeds and serve.

Morrocan Chicken Tagine

Traditional North African dish

Prep Time	Cook Time	Total Time	Servings
15 mins	45 mins	1 hr	**4 - 6**

Ingredients

8 chicken thighs (trimmed of fat) with skin on and bone in
2 leeks (top 2/3 only sliced crossways into 1/4 inch slices)
2 - 3 small preserved lemons (roughly chopped) or the zest and juice of 1 large or 2 small lemons
1 teaspoon paprika
1 teaspoon ground cumin
1/4 teaspoon cayenne pepper
1/2 teaspoon ground ginger
1/2 teaspoon ground coriander
1/4 teaspoon ground cinnamon
¼ teaspoon saffron strands
Salt and ground black pepper
1 tablespoon olive oil)or garlic infused olive oil)
1 x 400g cans cooked chickpeas (drained and rinsed)
500 millilitres GaF chicken stock
50 grams golden sultanas
2 large or 3 medium carrots, peeled and cut crosswise into1 cm chunks
70 grams pitted green olives
2 tablespoons honey
Fresh Coriander to garnish

Method

1. Slice the leeks
2. Zest and juice the lemon.
3. Combine the spices in a small bowl and set aside.
4. Season both sides of chicken pieces with 2 tspns salt and ½ teaspoon pepper.
5. Heat the oil on high heat in a large heavy-bottomed Dutch oven or pan until it begins to smoke.
6. Brown the chicken pieces, skin side down, in single layer until deep golden, about 5 minutes.
7. Using tongs, flip the chicken pieces over and brown the other side.
8. Reduce the heat to medium.
9. Add the leek and cook, stirring, until they are translucent 5 to 7 minutes.
10. Add the spices and cook, stirring constantly, until fragrant (30 secs).
11. Stir in the broth, half of the lemon zest, and ¼ teaspoon salt, scraping the bottom of the pan with a wooden spoon to loosen any browned bits.
12. Return the chicken (with any accumulated juices) to the pan, reduce the heat to medium-low, cover and simmer for 10 mins.
13. Add the chick peas cover, and simmer until the chicken is cooked through and the carrots are tender-crisp, about 10 mins more.
14. Stir in the olives, reserved lemon zest, coriander and 1 tblspn of lemon juice.
15. Remove the skin and bones and discard.
16. Taste the sauce and adjust seasoning with salt, pepper, and more lemon juice, if needed.
17. Serve with couscous.

Cooking & Eating in a Garlic-Free Zone

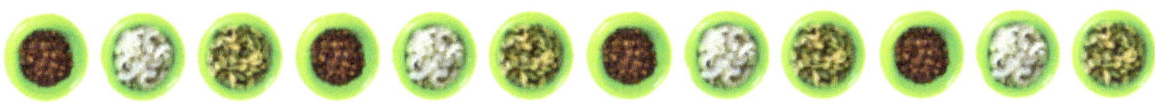

What is a tagine

A tagine, sometimes spelled "tajine," is a traditional Moroccan cooking pot made of ceramic or unglazed clay with a round base and low sides.

A cone-shaped cover sits on the base during cooking. The lid traps steam during cooking, cools it and returns the liquid to the clay pot, resulting in a moist dish with concentrated flavors.

I don't have a tagine. What can I use?

This recipe can be made in a dutch oven, which will give you the same effect of returning the liquid back to the pot to concentrate the deliciousness.

Or, you can use a large heavy based saucepan with a lid. One the ingredients are all in the pot, place two layers of baking paper over the top of the pot and fit the lid. It will give a good seal to keep the liquid in the pot.

Hummus
Middle Eastern favourite

Prep Time	Cook Time	Total Time	Servings
Overnight soak	1 hr 10min	1 hr 10 mins	N/A

1 cup of dried chickpeas soaked overnight.
1 cup of tahini
½ cup of lemon juice (or to taste)
1 teaspoon of salt
pinch of paprika (or to taste)
Extra virgin olive oil to drizzle on top
Chopped parsley to garnish.

You can make hummus using tinned chick peas. Not quite as tasty but great for a quick and easy dip!

1. Drain, rinse and place chickpeas in a heavy pot cover with cold water.
2. Cover with a lid leaving space for steam to escape
3. Bring to the boil, simmer for 1 hour or until the chickpeas are soft and the skins separate.
4. Drain off the chickpeas - remove skin.
5. Transfer to a food processor/blender
6. Add the tahini, lemon juice, salt and at ¼ to ½ a cup of water. Blend.
7. If the hummus is too thick, add more water until it is the consistency you want.

Beetroot Hummus
A different hummus flavour, sweet and luscious

Prep Time	Cook Time	Total Time	Servings
10 mins	5 mins	15 mins	N/A

Ingredients
1 x 400gm tin chickpeas, drained and rinsed
1 small raw red beetroot, roughly chopped
¼ tspn Asafoetida
1 tsp cumin
½ lemon, squeezed
1–2 tblspn runny tahini
¼–½ cup water
Himalayan sea salt

Method
1. Add all ingredients to a high speed blender and process until smooth and creamy, adding more water as needed to reach desired consistency.
2. Taste and add more lemon, tahini, Himalayan sea salt, or asafoetida to taste. (Careful with the Asafoetida!)
3. Serve as dip for your favorite veggies, crackers, or carrot chips!

Store leftover hummus in the fridge for up to one week.

Felafels

Lebanon's favourite street food. GaF but contains onion

Prep Time	Cook Time	Total Time	Servings
15 mins + resting	10 mins	25 mins + resting	Varies by size

Ingredients

1 cup dried chickpeas
1 cup peeled dried broad beans
3 tspns bicarbonate of soda
1 small onion
1 tspn garlic infused olive oil
2 handfuls parsley
1 handful fresh coriander
1 tsp Baharat
1 tsp dried coriander
1/2 tsp red chilli powder
1/2 tsp black pepper
1/2 tsp cumin powder
1 tbsp salt
Sesame seeds for dipping
Vegetable oil for deep frying

Method

1. In separate bowls, cover the chickpeas and broad beans with water.
2. Add a teaspoon of bicarbonate to each bowl and mix well.
3. Soak overnight.
4. The next day, rinse the beans in clear running water and set aside.
5. In a food processor, pulse the chickpeas and broad beans in batches until you have a medium coarse texture.
6. Transfer to a large mixing bowl.
7. Add the onion, coriander and parsley to the food processor and blitz.
8. Add to the bowl with the chickpeas and broad beans and mix well.
9. Add the spices, salt, 1 tspn of bicarbonate of soda and the garlic infused olive oil. The mix should not be dry.
10. Place in the refrigerator for an hour.
11. Shape your falafel into 'golf balls'.
12. Press them lightly into a plate of sesame seeds.
13. Heat up enough vegetable oil for deep frying.
14. Fry until golden (about 7 mins).
15. Serve with some tahini sauce and fresh pickles and vegetables in a wrap.

You can replace the onion with celery or crushed nigella seeds.

Cabbage Rolls

Leeks and garlic infused olive oil (optional) replace garlic

Prep Time	Cook Time	Total Time	Servings
70 mins	90 mins	2 hrs 40 mins	6

Ingredients
1 Cabbage head (2 kg)
300gm of lean ground beef
1 cup of rice, rinsed, dried
1 tblspn Garlic Infused olive oil (optional)
Green tops of 3 leeks
4 lemons, freshly squeezed
1-2 teaspoons of Baharat
2 tblspns of olive oil
Salt to taste

You will need two pots;
1. A large stock pot to separate the cabbage leaves
2. A wide and deep cooking pot for the rolls

Prepare the Cabbage
A 2kg cabbage head should yield around 30-35 rolled cabbage leaves depending on how big the leaves are.

Peel and discard the outer leaves of the cabbage., Then cut out the large stem from the bottom of the cabbage.

To separate the leaves, simmer the entire cabbage head in a large pot of boiling water for 5-10 minutes while carefully turning it over.

As the leaves loosen, pin down the cabbage inside the pot with one fork, and with another fork slowly and carefully peel away the leaves one after the other.

Place the cabbage leaves in a colander as you peel them. Once you've separated all leaves, try to roll one or two of them to see if they are soft enough. If they tear or break, put them back in the boiling water pot and cook for another 5 minutes.

Method
1. Mix the beef, the rice, 1 to 2 tspns of Baharat (or Mixed Spice) and ½ teaspoon of salt. Mix them well and set aside.
2. Start with the greenest leaves as they need more heat and longer to cook.
3. Lay each cabbage leaf separately on a cutting board, cut out the stem if it's too thick.
4. Spread 1-2 tblspns of meat stuffing along the edge of the leaf. Roll it slowly and tightly over the meat all the way.
5. Place the rolls in the pot side by side in a line until you've completed a layer.
6. Roll all the leaves and place them in the pot in this manner. You may have 2- 4 layers of rolls, depending on the width of the pot.
7. In a frying pan, sauté the leek in the olive oil, add a tblspn of lemon juice . Pour the mixture on top of rolls.
8. Mix remaining lemon juice with 4 cups of water, and ½-1 tspn of salt. Add this to the pot. The sauce should cover the rolls., If not add more water.
9. Carefully tilt the cooking pot a few times to ensure the sauce seeps through all layers.
10. Place a heavy plate on top of the rolls, cover the pot, and turn the stove to high heat until the pot boils, then turn heat to very low and allow to simmer 1 to 1½ hours (until the cabbage is no longer crunchy).
11. Serve hot with plain Greek yogurt and a squeeze of lemon juice.

Your Own Recipes

Cooking & Eating in a Garlic-Free Zone

Ingredients | *Method*

Ingredients | Method

Cooking & Eating in a Garlic-Free Zone

Ingredients | *Method*

Cooking & Eating in a Garlic-Free Zone

Ingredients   *Method*

Ingredients

Method

Resources, useful websites, and Attributions

Resources

1. Monashfodmap.com. 2021. Low FODMAP Diet | IBS Research at Monash University - Monash FODMAP. [online] Available at: https://www.monashfodmap.com/ [Accessed 19 October 2021]

2. Monash FODMAP App - available from Apple Store, Google Play for your phone/tablet.

3. https://www.monashfodmap.com/ibs-central/i-have-ibs/get-the-app/

4. Converting recipes from US and British books and websites is made much easier when you can do a quick conversion on your phone or iPad. This site is a Godsend. https://www.convertunits.com/

Useful Websites

- The Food Intolerance Dietician - very informative.
  https://www.thefoodintolerancedietitian.com.au/
  https://www.thefoodintolerancedietitian.com.au/post/onion-garlic-and-the-low-fodmap-diet

- The NSW Department of Health - information and diet help for garlic and onion intolerance and allergy.
  https://aci.health.nsw.gov.au/projects/diet-specifications/adult/allergy/no-garlic-strict

- The Healthful Clinic - a great explanation of the cause of garlic intolerance and the difference between fructans and fructose
  https://www.healthfulclinic.com.au/digestive-health/fructose-malabsorption/

Attributions

- 2021. chicken cacciatore. [image] Available at: <https://www.flickr.com/photos/pocketcultures/4256350030/> [Accessed 22 October 2021].

- 2021 Tandoor. [image] Available at https://en.wikipedia.org/ {accessed 4 December 2021]

- MussakasMeKolokithakiaKePatates.jpg. (n.d.). [Image]. https://upload.wikimedia.org/wikipedia/commons/thumb/9/9b/ {accessed 4 December 2021]

- 640px-Luxury_tandoor.png. (n.d.). [Image]. http://www.pixabay.com {accessed 4 December 2021]

- 1024px-Various_böreks_in_Turkey.jpg. (n.d.). [Image]. https://upload.wikimedia.org/wikipedia/commons/thumb/1/14/Various_böreks_in_Turkey.jpg/1024px-Various_böreks_in_Turkey.jpg {accessed 4 December 2021]

- 4256350030_911fa1e5ac_c.jpg. (n.d.). [Image]. http://www.pixabay.com {accessed 4 December 2021]

- 49066828568_b0486dc447_w.jpg. (n.d.). [Image]. http://www.pixabay.com {accessed 4 December 2021]

- aloo_gobi.jpg. (n.d.). [Image]. https://live.staticflickr.com 1110/3170159574_ae9b961552_b.jpg {accessed 4 December 2021]

- aubergine-89044_640.tiff. (n.d.). [Image]. http://www.pixabay.com {accessed 4 December 2021]

- Bamboo steamer.jpg https://images.victoriasbasement.com.au/ProductImages/images/1_80139_800_800.jpg {accessed 4 December 2021]

- Biryani_Home.jpg. (n.d.). [Image]. https://upload.wikimedia.org/wikipedia/commons/3/35/Biryani_Home.jpg

- bread-5471408_640.jpg. (n.d.). [Image]. Http://www.pixabay.com

- cashew-1802360.jpg. (n.d.-b). [Image]. http://www.pixabay.com

- DeLuvio, C. (n.d.). charles-deluvio-l7JScBIkfjY-unsplash.jpg [Image]. http://www.unsplash.com

- chili-pepper-5105059_640.jpg. (n.d.). [Image]. http://www.pixabay.com

- Chinese_Chicken_Chow_Mein.JPG. (n.d.). [Image]. https://upload.wikimedia.org/wikipedia/commons/e/e6/Chinese_Chicken_Chow_Mein.JPG

- chook.jpg. (n.d.). [Image]. https://encrypted-tbn0.gstatic.com/images?q=tbn:ANd9GcRZZCI2oqYVuq3v-06t40wH76TlLJ-FheRdWA&usqp=CAU

Cooking & Eating in a Garlic-Free Zone

- cooking-1835369_640.jpg. (n.d.). [Image]. http://www.pixabay.com

- cuscus-5371034_1280.jpg. (n.d.). [Image]. http://www.pixabay.com

- Easy-Beet-Hummus-6-150x150.jpg. (n.d.). [Image]. https://752867.smushcdn.com/1319836/wp-content/uploads/2018/08/Easy-Beet-Hummus-6-150x150.jpg?lossy=0&strip=1&webp=1

- eggplant-6136659_640.jpg. (n.d.). [Image]. https://pixabay.com/photos/eggplant-food-vegetable-produce-6136659/

- falafel-1088440_1920.jpg. (n.d.). [Image]. https://pixabay.com/photos

- falafel-5203363_640.jpg. (n.d.). [Image]. https://pixabay.com/photos

- Best-fatteh-in-Dubai.jpg. (n.d.). [Image]. https://www.sajway.com/blog/wp-content/uploads/2021/03/Best-fatteh-in-Dubai.jpg

- Headshot_FODMAP-Friendly.png. (n.d.). [Logo]. https://everydaynutrition.com.au/wp-content/uploads/2019/01/Headshot_FODMAP-Friendly.png

- Camalich, S. (n.d.). sergio-camalich-fUOTIfOIR-Q-unsplash.tiff [Image]. https://www.unsplash.com

- souvlaki-1649221_1920.jpg. (n.d.). [Image]. http://www.pixabay.com

- spaghetti-food-italian-pasta-fork-1549324. (n.d.). [Image]. https://pixabay.com/photos/spaghetti-food-italian-pasta-fork-1549324/

- spices-438527_640.jpg. (n.d.). [Image]. https://pixabay.com

- spices-cook-spice-up-ingredients-3811729. (n.d.). [Image]. https://pixabay.com/photos/spices-cook-spice-up-ingredients-3811729/

- spices-4082740.jpg. (n.d.). [Image]. https://pixabay.com/photos/spices-4082740/

- spreading-sweet-potatoes-on-shepherds-pie-560x373.jpg. (n.d.). [Image]. https://anothermusicinadifferentkitchen.com/wp-content/uploads/2019/07/spreading-sweet-potatoes-on-shepherds-pie-560x373.jpg

- spring-rolls-468156_640.jpg. (n.d.). [Image]. https://pixabay.com/photos/spring-rolls-468156_640/

- wok-265566_640.jpg. (n.d.). [Image]. https://pixabay.com/photos/wok-265566_640/

- wonton.jpg. (n.d.). [Image]. https://live.staticflickr.com/7854/47018544172_f946d354f6_b.jpg

- Image https://pixabay.com/users/engin_akyurt-3656355

- Image pocketcultures, [n.d.] [Image] https://creativecommons.org/licenses/by/2.0, via Wikimedia Commons

Cooking & Eating in a Garlic-Free Zone

- Atelier Joly Fish Pie -[n.d.] [image] https://commons.wikimedia.org/w/index.php?curid=70100

- Potato Gratin [n.d.] [Image] https://pixabay.com/users/suppenkasper-1357

- Tomato and sauce [n.d.] [image] Steve Buissinne [n.d.] https://pixabay.com_885168

- Tesa Robbins [n.d.] [image] https://pixabay.com_1638826

www.ingramcontent.com/pod-product-compliance
Ingram Content Group UK Ltd.
Pitfield, Milton Keynes, MK11 3LW, UK
UKHW061212180426
11947UKWH00029B/2014